AFRO-AMERICANS AND AFRICA

African Bibliographic Center
Special Bibliographic Series
New Series

Series Editor: Daniel G. Matthews

American-Southern African Relations: Bibliographic Essays
Mohamed A. El-Khawas and Francis A. Kornegay, Jr.

A Short Guide to the Study of Ethiopia: A General Bibliography
Alula Hidaru and Dessalegn Rahmato

Somalia: A Bibliographical Survey
Mohamed Khalief Salad

African Bibliographic Center ● Special Bibliographic Series
New Series ● Number 3

AFRO-AMERICANS AND AFRICA

Black Nationalism at the Crossroads

Compiled by

WILLIAM B. HELMREICH

GREENWOOD PRESS

Westport, Connecticut ● London, England

Library of Congress Cataloging in Publication Data

Helmreich, William B
    Afro-Americans and Africa.

    (Special bibliographic series - African Bibliographic Center ;
new ser., no. 3)
    Includes index.
    1. Afro-Americans—Bibliography. 2. Africa—Bibliography.
I. Title. II. Series: African Bibliographic Center. Special bibliographic
series ; new ser., no. 3.
Z3507.A45 N.S., no. 3 [Z1361.N39] [E185]
ISBN 0-8371-9439-3 016.96s [016.973'04'96073]

                                      76-56621

Library of Congress Catalog Card Number: 76-56621
ISBN 0-8371-9439-3

First Published in 1977

Greenwood Press, Inc.,
51 Riverside Avenue, Westport, Connecticut 06880

Printed in the United States of America

278706

CONTENTS

SERIES FOREWORD

The Center cannot claim to have published this bibliographical data on the historical development of relations between Afro-Americans and Africans in a mood of detachment. The existing need for works of this nature, and during this particular juncture in time with America's Bicentennial and the significant thrust for a constituency for African issues in the U.S. during a presidential election year, is obvious. These key factors, among many, many others, offer a clear rationale for an illustrative and explanatory bibliographical tool of current research sources.

It is hoped that this guide will also be of use to the new student of Afro-American-African relations. Unfortunately, it is still possible to encounter many persons who are totally unaware of the depth of the continuing relationships between Africans and those of African descent the world over. On the other hand, one has only to scan the vast array of research documented in our quarterly journal "A Current Bibliography on African Affairs," under the section *African Heritage Studies,* to recognize that there now exists a considerable body of scholars and individuals who now place significant emphasis on things African and Africa's "natural" constituency in the U.S.

Many of the views presented in Helmreich's work can be interpreted as signs of health. It is quite natural that there should be a considerable divergence of opinion among those devoted to the development of improved relations between Africa and the U.S. and to determining the directions in which these relations should move.

Daniel G. Matthews

Washington, D.C.
August 1976

FOREWORD

Attempts to portray the attitudes of Afro-Americans toward Africa and its people are fraught with difficulties because these attitudes are kaleidoscopic and often chameleon-like in nature. But more importantly, these attitudes are operational weapons. In a Heisenbergian manner, simply by discussing the reasons for these attitudes, people change their very basis for them, thereby making conclusions meaningless or, what is more likely, simply wrong.

The attitudes of Afro-Americans toward their ancestral homeland are usually tinged with aspects of pride and prejudice. Yet the very acknowledgement or revelation of their nature creates tension. The reason is that the context in which people discuss the attitudes of Afro-Americans toward Africa--a world still dominated by European peoples who continue to hold African peoples in contempt--is basically unacceptable to blacks. The result is that many Afro-Americans view and use their attitudes about Africa as a means for coping with or challenging the basic thesis of world-wide white domination. This should not be surprising since whites (who are often inordinately interested in Afro-American attitudes toward Africa) also attempt to use these attitudes as a means of maintaining their own hegemony. Given these conditions, it is understandable why there is great uncertainty as to the real attitudes of Afro-Americans toward the land of their ancestors.

While Afro-Americans have maintained an interest in Africa over centuries, the present generation of Afro-Americans has more contact with or relations with that continent than any other group of blacks since the end of the slave trade. Except for black intellectuals and missionaries the African continent remained for most blacks a land of drums and shadows. Paul Cuffee did initiate an exodus that eventually led thousands to recross the Atlantic, but most black freedmen felt that they should not leave their brethren in thralldom and forget the sacrifices that their ancestors had made to develop the United States of America. The argument about whether to return to Africa or to seek salvation in America would rage between Delaney and Douglass, and while it was muted between Booker T. Washington and W.E.B. Du Bois, Marcus A. Garvey did attract much attention with his "Back to Africa" movement. Booker T. Washington was too busy to go to Africa, but sent agronomists there and was rewarded by schools built in his honor. Garvey did not get to Africa, but his messianic dreams would later help bring freedom to the continent. Ironically, it was DuBois, the ideologue, who did not dream of returning to Africa, who found refuge and finally the peace of the grave in that continent.

Following on the heels of Du Bois, literally hundreds of Afro-Americans make the pilgrimage to Africa each year. Each in his or her own way views that continent and its people through a rather personal prism and attempts to come to grips with the past. The more articulate among them attempt to express the meaning of their saga and their longing, but even these often subjugate their true feelings to their perception of how best to use their attitudes in the historic battle for Afro-American freedom.

It is true, as William B. Helmreich states, that the numerous books and articles written about Afro-American attitudes toward Africa during 1960-1973 reflected a period of rapid change called the Second Reconstruction. As during the first Reconstruction, Afro-Americans heralded the 1960s with great hopes for making significant strides toward freedom and equality in America. The more perceptive among them now realize that the major reason that the first Reconstruction failed was because at that time Western Europe was in the process of dominating the globe, and would eventually conquer and colonize Africa. Therefore, it was almost impossible for white Americans who had inherited the mantle of European world hegemony to grant full equality to their former slaves. The Second Reconstruction is occurring at a very different period in the world's history; the end of the Western Era. While few blacks during the first Reconstruction epoch saw their future linked to that of Africa, the Afro-Americans during the Second Reconstruction recognize a definite connection between their Sit-Ins and Civil Rights marches, and the lowering of foreign flags at midnight in many an African state. The Nixon era brought with it "benign neglect" and a retreat from the promises of the 1960s, and the "time of troubles" in the fledgling African states suggested that the black world faced the end of the Second Reconstruction. However, Nixon and his clique have passed into the limbo of history. The African revolution has continued and the Afro-Americans are moving from the rhetoric of the 1960s to political action in the 1970s. Due in part to strong pressure from articulate black statesmen and scholars, the architect of recent U.S. foreign policy toward Africa, Dr. Kissinger, was forced to go to the continent and, while there, preach the Afro-American slogan of majority rule for the Africans in Africa. Can white Americans ignore the implications of this for the future of Afro-Americans in America?

William B. Helmreich ought to be congratulated for putting together this work entitled <u>Afro-Americans and Africa: Black Nationalism at the Crossroads</u>. He has rendered a great service to both the academic and lay public for collecting information about the important books and articles that were written about Afro-Americans and Africa during this exciting but often frustrating period. His decision to include in the bibliography scholarly treatises as well as popular articles is to be applauded since so many different kinds of Americans are now involved with Africa. Academics as well as lay persons will profit from having at their disposal a handy annotated reference work in which they can find an entire spectrum of the opinions of Afro-American attitudes about Africa and their relations with that continent. They will be pleasantly surprised to find that so many persons were writing about Afro-Americans and Africa during this period and that their views varied so widely.

The compiler tells us that he views this contribution as only a point of departure for future bibliographers. Let us hope that he will prepare a definitive volume on this important period when black nationalism found itself at the crossroads. That work could well be one of a whole series of bibliographies dealing with the evolving nature of attitudes of Afro-Americans to Africa.

Elliott P. Skinner
Columbia University

Probably no other period in American history can compare to that
of the 1960s in so far as the development of Black pride and
identity is concerned. During those years Afro-Americans became
involved in a variety of programs and activities ranging from
revolutionary socialism and community control, to Black capitalism. Among the important developments in this era was a considerable increase in identification with Africa. This interest
manifested itself in many areas, including the spread of Black
studies programs emphasizing African history, politics and culture, the adoption of African modes of dress, and visits to
Africa by more and more Black Americans.

One indication of the growing interest in this topic has been
the tremendous interest, within the last decade or so, of books
and articles, both scholarly and popular, that deal with the
relationships of Afro-Americans in the United States to Africa.
Unfortunately, the work in this area has not been systematically
brought together and evaluated in a comprehensive and thorough
manner. This introductory essay evaluates research done in the
last decade or so on the historical basis of this relationship.
Its purpose, however, is not to offer a critique of the literature but rather to serve as a useful guide to interested scholars
and educators by presenting the best material available in this
area and to introduce the larger and more detailed bibliography
that is the subject of this book. Specifically, the period
covered is from 1960 to 1973, a period that saw millions of
Black people actively engaged in a struggle to improve the quality of their lives in every possible way. In so far as it served
to enhance Black pride, awareness, and identity, the increased
interest in Africa that developed during these years must be
seen as a direct and important result of that struggle.

General Works

Although no book has yet been written that fully describes and
assesses the history of the Afro-American's involvement with
the African continent, a number of excellent articles summarizing
such interest have appeared in recent years. Two of the best
articles have been written by E.P. Skinner and St. Clair Drake.[1]
Both writers do a thorough job of tracing the history of the
Black community's involvement with Africa and are therefore
excellent starting points for the reader interested in this topic.

Turning to edited works, a very good collection compiled by
Martin Kilson and Adelaide Hill presents many important documents
which graphically demonstrate the important role played by Africa
over the years in the Black community.[2] Included are selections
from the works of Martin Delaney, Alexander Crummell, Paul
Robeson, Alain Locke, and many others. This is a comprehensive
and well-balanced collection, although it could have benefited
considerably from the inclusion of more selections reflecting
the recent upsurge of interest in this subject. Another useful

collection has been edited by John A. Davis, former Executive
Director of the American Society for African Culture (AMSAC).[3]
The first two portions of this compilation deal with African
society and culture while the third section is devoted to an
examination of attitudes toward Africa. Among the topics discussed are an evaluation of the role played by the NAACP in
advancing knowledge about Africa,[4] an article by E. Franklin
Frazier concerning the role that Afro-Americans can play in
Africa,[5] and two interesting contributions on Liberia.[6] A third
anthology by Okon E. Uya, while it contains a few good selections,
consists mostly of articles that are well-known and already
widely published.[7]

The Nineteenth Century

When we think of migration to Africa, Liberia is often the first
country that comes to mind. Interest in Sierra Leone, however,
while not as great as that shown in Liberia, preceded the interest
that developed in Liberia. Among those from the New World who
migrated to Sierra Leone was a group of 1190 ex-slaves who had
been freed by the British, had resettled in Nova Scotia, and who
had eventually gone to Sierra Leone. Other emigrants to Sierra
Leone came from the United States via England. These migrations
are detailed in an authoritative history of Sierra Leone, written
by Christopher Fyfe.[8] One American who left the United States
in 1815 for Sierra Leone was the well-known Black merchant, Paul
Cuffe. One of the best biographies of this individual has been
written by Sheldon H. Harris, whose book includes a record of
Cuffe's diary and his letters.[9]

The emigrationist Martin R. Delaney was probably one of the most
important Black leaders of the Nineteenth Century. While the
reader has much to choose from here, perhaps the two best (and
most readable) works on this figure are the ones by Victor Ullman
and by Dorothy Sterling.[10] Those interested only in Delaney's
trip to the Niger Valley are directed to articles by A.H.M. Kirk-
Greene and by Howard H. Bell.[11] Bell makes a number of interesting
points in his evaluation of sentiment for emigration during the
1858-61 period, particularly in assessing the attitudes of Delaney
and Frederick Douglass. He argues that had it not been for the
ourbreak of the Civil War, Douglass would probably have become
a strong supporter of emigration as a solution to the problems
then facing Black people in the United States.

Another articulate spokesman for Black emigration was Bishop
Alexander Crummell. Good overviews of Crummell's life and ideas
may be found in an article by Katherine O. Wahle and in a Ph.D.
dissertation by O.M. Scruggs.[12] It is unfortunate that relatively
little attention seems to have been paid to this important Nineteenth Century leader and his contributions to the development
and awakening of Black consciousness in America.

By way of contrast a good deal of solid research is available
on the life and work of Edward Wilmot Blyden. The best book-
length work has been written by Hollis R. Lynch and is a valuable

source of information for both the beginner and the scholar.[13]
Another good book on Blyden has been done by Edith Holden,
although, as the author acknowledges, it is not so much an
analysis of Blyden's life and work as it is a straightforward
factual biography.[14] An intriguing article by Thomas H. Henriksen
examines Blyden's writings in terms of how they influence Blacks
today.[15] In it Henriksen asserts that Blyden's ideas on "Pan-
Negroism" were the basis for what later became Pan-Africanism (as
Lynch has also noted) and that his ideas on Black pride were
actually the precursors of the "Black is beautiful" idea.

Yet another important leader of the Nineteenth Century was Bishop
Henry M. Turner. In a well-written and well-documented book,
Edwin S. Redkey chronicles the life of Turner and the involvement of the American Colonization Society with emigration to
Africa.[16] Redkey's thought-provoking work does an excellent job
of covering the crucial period between 1890 and 1910, a period
that witnessed the emergence of two of the most important leaders
in the history of the Afro-American experience ---- Booker T.
Washington and W.E.B. DuBois.

The Twentieth Century

Probably the best introductions to interest in Africa during the
Twentieth Century have been written by St. Clair Drake and Robert
G. Weisbord.[17] Drake discusses the concepts of Negritude,
cultural and political Pan-Africanism, and the effects these
movements have had and are likely to have upon Afro-Americans in
the future. He seems to feel that Africa's significance for the
Afro-American lies primarily in its ability to fulfill the psychological needs of Black people in terms of developing pride in
their history and culture. Drake observes that while Africa will
probably be hospitable to those few who come to Africa to settle,
it is unlikely that Africa will actively solicit emigration from
the United States. Considering that Drake's article first
appeared in 1963, it was almost prophetic in predicting the
current increase of interest in Africa and the attitudes that
have come to be associated with such interest.

Weisbord's book contains an excellent discussion of interest in
Africa from the beginning of the Twentieth Century to the present.
In addition, Weisbord presents in-depth analyses of pro-Ethiopian
sentiment in the Black community, the Garvey Movement, and a
fascinating chapter describing the many, yet little-known
Africanist groups that sprang up in the years following Garvey's
demise. Weisbord also evaluates current interest in Africa and
the attitudes of Africans toward such interest. Another useful
introduction to the subject of expatriation in recent times may
be found in an article by Leonard E. Collins Jr., in which the
author focuses on contemporary interest in Africa and the expectations of Blacks who have recently gone there.[18]

One of the focal points in the Black community's involvement
with things African has been Ethiopia. In a highly readable,
informative, and well-documented article, Weisbord presents a

detailed account of this involvement, discussing not only the
interest evinced in Ethiopia during its war with Italy, but also
the important place occupied by Ethiopia in the Afro-American
community before the 1930s.[19] Weisbord observes that this interest was due mainly to two factors --- Ethiopia's long cultural
tradition and its resistance to European colonization and domination.

Thoughts about Black leaders who stressed ties with Africa often
lead to Marcus Garvey and W.E.B. Du Bois rather than to Booker T.
Washington. Therefore, Louis R. Harlan's excellent article
detailing Washington's involvement with Africa is most welcome
and worth while.[20] In his essay Harlan touches upon various
aspects of this relationship, including Washington's efforts to
convince President Theodore Roosevelt to improve the conditions
of Black people living in the Congo, his attempts to prevent
Liberia from being swallowed up by European colonialists, and
the sending of Tuskegeeans to Togo as farmers in the beginning
of the Twentieth Century. Harlan asserts, however, that Washington's conservatism was reflected in his views on Africa and that,
in principle at least, he supported colonialism by encouraging
American investment in Africa.

One of the most important centers for Black culture in America
during the early part of the Twentieth Century was, of course,
Harlem, and a great deal has been written on that community.[21]
These works all deal, to some extent, with interest in Africa as
it was expressed by leaders and members of the Harlem community.
Nathan I. Huggins, in particular, portrays the Harlem community
in terms of its personality, including in this portrayal a dis-
cussion of how various Harlem Renaissance figures such as Alain
Locke, Aaron Douglas, Countee Cullen, and Langston Hughes viewed
the African continent.[22] In an article published in 1963,
Richard B. Moore has also given us a vivid picture of the role
played by Africa in the minds of Harlemites from the turn of the
Century to today's times.[23] In addition to discussing Garvey,
Du Bois, and Ethiopia, Moore also talks about the reaction in
Harlem to the 1956 Arab-Israeli War and gives us a good descrip-
tion of the various Africa-oriented groups that have flourished
in Harlem from the 1920s until today.

In response, perhaps, to the renewed interest in Marcus Garvey
during the 1960s, a good deal of material has appeared recently
on the life and activities of this pivotal and controversial
leader. No less than three solid biographies and a number of
excellent articles were published in this period. While some
may question the seriousness of Garvey's intentions regarding
African settlement, a careful reading of Amy Jacque Garvey's
book leaves little doubt as to Garvey's contributions in giving
publicity to Africa and in making Black people prouder of their
African heritage.[24] Theodore G. Vincent's account, in addition
to its careful description of Garvey's life, contains an especially interesting section on the Universal Negro Improvement
Association's influence on later nationalism.[25] Vincent talks
about what happened to the Garveyites and the leaders of the

U.N.I.A. after the Movement collapsed, what groups they joined, and how effective they were. Elton Fax's biography treats Garvey's life in the context of West Indian, particularly Jamaican history.[26] Written in an interesting style, Fax draws heavily upon earlier works by Edmund David Cronon and others in interpreting various aspects of Garvey's life and career.[27] For those interested in a first-hand examination of Garvey's writings, the standard work is Amy Jacque Garvey's <u>Philosophy and Opinions of Marcus Garvey</u>, which was originally published in two separate volumes, the first appearing in 1923 and the second in 1925.[28] The second edition of this work, published in 1967, is prefaced by an excellent introduction written by E.U. Essien-Udom summarizing Garvey's life.

A well-documented article by M.B. Akpan presents a detailed discussion of Garvey's plan to settle Afro-Americans in Liberia, with special emphasis upon the reasons for Liberia's negative response to his efforts.[29] In a thought-provoking article critical of Garvey, Wilson Moses asserts that Garvey merely capitalized on Black pride, displayed an elitist view towards Africa, and was uninterested in "uncivilized areas" there except for the purpose of "redeeming" them.[30] In arguing that W.E.B. Du Bois and Malcolm X were far more important for the development of Black nationalism, Moses also suggests that the disillusionment that followed Garvey's conviction may have be responsible for the expansion of a generally negative attitude towards Black nationalism that prevailed in the Black community for a number of years after the Garvey era.

Turning to the crucial role of W.E.B. Du Bois in promoting interest in Africa, we have an article written by Harold R. Isaacs which argues that although Du Bois was "a romantic racist", he never urged mass migration to Africa.[31] Rather, asserts Isaacs, he concentrated on promoting the freedom of Africa for <u>Africans</u>. The article is based on an interview conducted with Du Bois. A number of other articles have appeared in recent years assessing Du Bois' involvement in Pan-Africanism.[32] These essays, most of which focus on his participation in the various Pan-African Congresses held between 1900 and 1945, leave no doubt as to the political and ideological importance of Du Bois' activities in this area. William L. Hansberry has written a fine article evaluating Du Bois' scholarly contributions to an understanding of Africa's past.[33] Hansberry's article is lucid and informative, particularly in his discussion of how he and other Black scholars were influenced by Du Bois' interest in this topic. In understanding why there is not a great deal of information on Du Bois' views concerning the relationship between Afro-Americans and Africa, it must be taken into account that when Du Bois died in 1963 the militant and nationalist phase of the Black Movement was not yet really under way. Moreover, although Du Bois was an advocate of closer ties between Black people in the United States and in Africa, this was only one of his many interests.

For a complete and accurate assessment of Malcolm X's role in history we will probably have to wait until the passage of time allows historians to place his contributions in a proper perspective. Nevertheless, it is already abundantly clear that Malcolm X played a central role in the development of Black nationalism and pride during the 1960s and that his influence continues to be felt in the Black community. Those interested in a general picture of his life are, of course, referred to the well-known Autobiography of Malcolm X and to the biography by Peter Goldman.[34] Although Malcolm X's own account presents a fascinating picture of his experience while in Africa, Goldman's book is also very useful because it gives us a sensitive and vivid portrayal of this great leader's ambivalencies and doubts on the question of just how Black people in the United States ought to develop their ties with their brothers throughout the world.

Finally we have an excellent collection of interpretive essays, interviews, speeches, etc., edited by John Henrik Clarke concerning Malcolm X.[35] Of particular interest for our topic are some of the speeches given by Malcolm X in which he talks about the importance of the African heritage, his attempts to forge a common Black front, and his plans for the organization which he founded, the Organization of Afro-American Unity.[36]

As this essay and the bibliography that follows demonstrate, a good deal of research has been carried out in recent years on the historical aspects of the Afro-American's relationship to Africa. It is important that such research continue, not only because of its scholarly value, but because Africa is today an important factor in the self-perception of many members of the Black community. Thus developing a better understanding of the Afro-American's past concern with Africa has important ramifications for the present as well.

Notes

1. E. P. Skinner, African, Afro-American, White American: A Case of Pride and Prejudice (New York: The Trustees of Columbia University, 1973), Pamphlet. S.C. Drake, "Negro Americans and the Africa Interest", in J.P. Davis (ed.) The American Negro Reference Book (Englewood Cliffs: Prentice-Hall, 1966), pp. 662-705.
2. M. Kilson and A.C. Hill (eds.), Apropos of Africa (New York: Anchor, 1971).
3. J.A. Davis (ed.), Africa Seen by American Negro Scholars (New York: American Society of African Culture, 1963).
4. J.W. Ivy, "Traditional NAACP Interest in Africa (as reflected in the pages of The Crisis)"in J.A. Davis, Ibid., pp. 229-246.
5. E.F. Frazier, "Potential American Negro Contributions to African Social Development," in J.A. Davis, Ibid., pp. 263-278.
6. W.E.B. Du Bois, "Liberia, the League and the United States." in J.A. Davis, Ibid., pp. 329-344; J.W. Davis, "Liberia, Past and Present," Op.Cit., pp. 344-359.
7. O.E. Uya (ed.), Black Brotherhood: Afro-Americans and Africa Lexington, Massachusetts: D.C. Heath, 1971).

8. C. Fyfe, A History of Sierra Leone (London: Oxford University Press, 1962).
9. S.H. Harris, Paul Cuffe: Black America and the African Return (New York: Simon and Schuster, 1972).
10. V. Ullman, Martin R. Delaney: The Beginnings of Black Nationalism (Boston: Beacon Press, 1971); D. Sterling, The Making of an Afro-American: Martin Robison Delaney, 1812-1885 (New York: Doubleday, 1971).
11. A.H.M. Kirk-Greene, "America in the Niger Valley: A Colonization Centenary," Phylon 23, Fall (1962), pp. 225-239; H.H. Bell, "Negro Nationalism: A Factor in Emigration Projects 1858-1861," Journal of Negro History 47, January (1962), pp. 42-53.
12. K.O. Wahle, "Alexander Crummell: Black Evangelist and Pan-Negro Partiot," Phylon 24, 4 (1968), pp. 388-395; O.M. Scruggs, We the Children of Africa in this Land: Alexander Crummell (Washington, D.C.: Howard University, 1972), Ph.D. Diss..
13. H.R. Lynch, Edward Wilmot Blyden: Pan-Negro Patriot, 1832-1912 (New York: Oxford University Press, 1967).
14, E. Holden, Blyden of Liberia: An Account of the Life and Labor of Edward Wilmot Blyden, L.L.D., as Recorded in Letters and in Print (New York: Vantage Press, 1966).
15. T.H. Henriksen, "Edward W. Blyden: His Influence on Contemporary Afro-Americans," Pan-African Journal 4, Summer (1971), pp. 255-265.
16. E. Redkey, Black Exodus: Black Nationalism and Back to Africa Movements 1890-1910 (New Haven: Yale University Press, 1969).
17. S.C. Drake, "'Hide my Face?' On Pan-Africanism and Negritude," in H. Hill (ed.) Soon One Morning (New York: Alfred A. Knopf, 1963), pp. 78-105; R.G. Weisbord, Ebony Kinship: Africa, Africans, and the Afro-American (Westport, Conn., 1973).
18. L.E. Collins Jr., "The Afro-American Return to Africa in the Twentieth Century --- Illusion and Reality," Afro-American Studies 3, 2 (1972), pp. 103-109.
19. R.G. Weisbord, "Black America and the Italian-Ethiopian Crisis: An Episode in Pan-Negroism," The Historian 34, 2 (1972), pp. 230-241.
20. L.B. Harlan, "Booker T. Washington and the White Man's Burden," American Historical Review 71, January (1966) pp. 441-467.
21. See J.W. Johnson, Black Manhattan, (New York: Atheneum, 1930); C. McKay, Harlem: Negro Metropolis, (New York: E.P. Dutton, 1940); G. Osofsky, Harlem: The Making of a Ghetto, (New York: Harper & Row, 1963); S.M. Scheiner, Negro Mecca: A History of the Negro in New York City, 1865-1920 (New York: New York University Press, 1965); N.I. Huggins, Harlem Renaissance (New York: Oxford University Press, 1971).
22. N.I. Huggins, Op. Cit., pp. 79-81; pp. 137-189.
23. R.B. Moore, "Africa Conscious Harlem," Freedomways 3, Summer (1963), pp. 315-334.
24. A.J. Garvey, Garvey and Garveyism (Kingston, Jamaica, 1963).
25. T.G. Vincent, Black Power and the Garvey Movement (Berkeley: Ramparts Press, 1970).

26. E. Fax, Garvey: The Story of a Pioneer Black Nationalist (New York: Dodd, Mead, 1972).

27. E.D. Cronon, Black Moses: The Story of Marcus Garvey and the Universal Negro Improvement Association (Madison: University of Wisconsin Press, 1955).

28. A.J. Garvey, The Philosophy and Opinions of Marcus Garvey (London: Frank Cass, 1967, 2 Volumes).

29. M.B. Akpan, "Liberia and the Universal Negro Improvement Association: The Background to the Abortion of Garvey's Scheme for African Colonization," Journal of African History, 14, 1 (1973), pp. 105-127.

30. W. Moses, "Marcus Garvey: A Reappraisal," Black Scholar 4, November-December (1972), pp. 38-49.

31. H.R. Isaacs, "Du Bois and Africa," Race 2, November (1960).

32. See B. Fonlon, "The Passing of a Great African," Freedomways 5, Winter (1965), pp. 195-206; R.B. Moore, "Du Bois and Pan Africa," Freedomways 5, Winter (1965), pp. 166-187; D. Walden and K. Wylie, "W.E.B. Du Bois: Pan-Africanism's Intellectual Father," Journal of Human Relations 14, 1 (1966), pp. 28-41. C.G. Contee, "The Emergence of Du Bois as an African Nationalist," Journal of Negro History 54, January (1969), pp. 48-63.

33. W.L. Hansberry, "W.E.B. Du Bois' Influence on African History," Freedomways 5, Winter (1965), pp. 73-87.

34. Malcolm X (with the assistance of A. Haley), The Autobiography of Malcolm X (New York: Grove Press, 1965); P. Goldman, The Death and Life of Malcolm X (New York: Harper & Row, 1973).

35. J.H. Clarke (ed.), Malcolm X: The Man and His Times (New York: Colliers, 1969).

36. Ibid., pp. 321-331, pp. 288-301, pp. 335-342.

ANTHROPOLOGICAL AND SOCIOLOGICAL INVESTIGATIONS:
AFRO-AMERICANS AND AFRICA

Introduction

There has been a tradition of continued interest in Africa within the black community dating from the time that African captives were first brought to the shores of what is today known as the United States. While such interest has always been present it has, however, ebbed and flowed in accordance with the changing fortunes of the blacks in America.

One of the earliest advocates of emigration to Africa was Paul Cuffe, a black shipowner from Massachusetts who sailed for Sierra Leone in 1815 with 38 other Afro-Americans. While it is not clear what proportion of the black population supported such efforts at the time, it is clear that Cuffe was not alone in his beliefs. The names of the earliest churches such as the African Methodist Episcopal and the Abyssinian Baptist churches bear testimony that Africa had not been forgotten by the black community. Moreover, as a number of writers (Stuckey, 1969; Blassingame, 1972; Rawick, 1972) have shown, a great deal of African culture was retained by many of the slaves who worked on the plantations.

By the 1850s a good number of black leaders had begun voicing their support of emigration as a solution to the injustices faced by many Afro-Americans in this country. Among the most famous advocates of this position were Martin R. Delany and Alexander Crummell. Delany was a physician who had visited Liberia and Nigeria and who was active in various colonization efforts until the outbreak of the Civil War. Bishop Crummell was probably the most important figure among black missionaries who were involved with Africa. What eventually became known as W.E.B. Du Bois' theory of the "talented tenth" was actually first developed by Crummell who agreed that the educated black elite in this country had a special obligation to help uplift the race.

Although interest in Africa waned somewhat following the end of the Civil War it enjoyed a revival in the 1880s, in large part because of the activities of Bishop Henry M. Turner. It was the force of Turner's personality and his abilities as an orator that were perhaps most responsible for keeping the spirit of black nationalism alive during the late nineteenth and early twentieth centuries. But perhaps the greatest leader in terms of forging ties between Afro-Americans and Africa was W.E.B. Du Bois who sponsored and participated in numerous conferences on Pan-Africanism (the first was held in London in 1900) and who made countless scholarly contributions toward a better understanding of Africa's past and present. Although Du Bois did not advocate a return to Africa he was committed to the belief that a powerful Africa would be of inestimable value to black people throughout the entire world.

Booker T. Washington is perhaps more often thought of as an

accommodationist than as a nationalist. Yet he too played an
important part in focusing the attention of the black community
on Africa. In addition to sending students from Tuskegee Institute to work in various parts of Africa, Washington also tried
to influence Theodore Roosevelt to improve the conditions of
blacks in the Congo. At the same time, as the historian Louis
Harlan (1966) has pointed out, Washington's conservatism extended
to his attitudes on Africa as well and, in principle at least, he
supported colonialism there.

A list of important figures in the black community who nurtured
and developed interest in Africa could easily fill several pages-
names such as Carter G. Woodson, Rayford Logan, Countee Cullen,
James Weldon Johnson, etc., but in terms of appeal to the black
masses of America, Marcus Mosiah Garvey had no equal. Through
his organization, the Universal Negro Improvement Association,
Garvey was able to fire the imagination of black people throughout the United States and imbue them with pride in and awareness
of their historical origins. Despite Garvey's lack of success in
his efforts to establish a colony in Liberia, there is little
doubt concerning Garvey's contribution in drawing attention to
Africa and the relationship of Afro-Americans to it.

Identification with Africa continued to be expressed by the black
community in a variety of ways in the years following Garvey's
demise. In 1935 the black community rallied to the support of
Ethiopia during the Italian-Ethiopian War. Mass rallies were
held, money was raised, and volunteers were recruited. In 1945
the Fifth Pan-African Congress was held in Manchester, England.
Although Du Bois was instrumental in organizing the meeting its
leadership was, for the first time, made up primarily of Africans,
many of whom were to see the initial realization of their goals
some twelve years later when Ghana became an independent state.

While the 1950s were perhaps characterized, on the whole, by
integrationist sentiment, the 1960s saw a considerable increase
of identification with Africa on the part of many Afro-Americans.
This interest manifested itself in many areas ranging from the
spread of black studies programs that included courses on Africa
and the formation of many organizations that focused on Africa,
to the adoption of African modes of dress and the popularity of
"Afro" haircuts. As the discussion until now has shown, such
interest has been a recurring theme throughout the history of the
black community in America although, perhaps, never before on
such a wide scale.

One indication of the interest in this field has been the tremendous increase in the last decade or so of books and articles, both
scholarly and popular, that deal with the relationships of Afro-
Americans to the African continent. For example, from 1950 to
1960 the New York Times carried less than 15 articles on this
topic while the period 1960-1972 saw the appearance of over 70
articles on the same subject. While most of these articles were
more journalistic than scholarly, the same trend was present in
academic journals where hundreds of articles in a wide range of

disciplines were published. This essay will discuss some of
the more important books and articles that have appeared in
recent years on the subject of Afro-Americans and Africa.
The period covered will be from 1960 to 1972, a period which
saw millions of black people in this country actively engaged
in a struggle to improve the quality of their lives in every
possible way. In addition, a bibliography of the relevant literature in this area, including works not touched upon in the
essay, appears at the end of the chapter.

General Works

The Myth of the Negro Past (1958) by Melville J. Herskovitz is
perhaps the classic work in the field of cultural relationships
between Afro-Americans and Africa. Originally published in 1941
(the 1958 edition contains a new preface by the author) this book
is basic reading for anyone seeking an understanding of the subject, hence its inclusion here despite its pre-1960 publication
date. Generally speaking, the book is a provocative, fascinating,
and wide-ranging discussion of African survivals among black
people in the New World. While many of Herskovitz' assertions
concerning retentions of Africanisms have been criticized as being
somewhat speculative, the work succeeds admirably in refuting the
then popularly held notion that African people had lost their
culture upon their arrival in the New World or had never possessed
a culture of their own. In a later article (1960) Herskovitz
replied sharply to his critics saying that it was ridiculous to
demand evidence of a perfect retention of an African behavior
pattern before accepting a New World cultural practice or charac-
teristic as being African in origin.

Another important work is Mantu: The New African Culture (1961)
by Jahnheinz Jahn, who makes a number of interesting observations
on the subject, espeically in his chapter on blues music. While
Jahn identifies a number of similarities between African and Afro-
American music he also points out that in African music the
singing accompanies the drums whereas in Afro-American blues the
opposite holds true: The singer leads and the instruments accompany (p. 221). Jahn also observes that Afro-American novels such
as Ellison's Invisible Man (1947), Wright's Native Son (1940) and
Baldwin's Go Tell it on the Mountain (1963) are not at all similar to African novels since they deal primarily with the problems
of split personalities and inferiority complexes that are particularly relevant to the black experience in America. If Jahn's
point was valid ten or fifteen years ago it is certainly no longer true today for we can see parallels and similarities in many
areas. For example, black South African writers such as Peter
Abrahams and Ezekiel Mphalele have written about the same problems
of discrimination that Afro-Americans were discussing in the
1960s. Works by Africans dealing with Negritude find their
equivalent in Afro-American analyses of Soul and its implications.
One observer has drawn some interesting comparisons between the
autobiographical writing of Afro-Americans and Africans (Bruchac,
1971) and there is an excellent book that deals exclusively with
Afro-American and African writings in a broad range of areas

(Cook and Henderson, 1969). On the whole, however, Jahnheinz Jahn's book is a valuable contribution towards an understanding of both African and Afro-American culture.

Roger Bastide's African Civilizations in the New World (1971), which originally appeared in French, is a third important work concerning African culture in the New World. In his discussion of religion Bastide makes a number of incisive points with regard to the United States. Although many patterns of behavior are unique to black Americans, the author asserts that they are often affected by a mentality that still retains African ways of thinking, i.e., a desire for group association. While Afro-Americans have borrowed from American revivalism (which originated in Scotland) in their religious behavior, there are some important differences between the two that may be a result of the African heritage. Some examples given by Bastide are: White revivalist groups have onlookers as well as performers while black groups consist exclusively of performers; among whites the movements are rather disorganized and jerky as opposed to the more rhythmic and coordinated movements of the black groups. At the same time Bastide notes that both the white revivalists and the black groups have influenced each other. The book also contains an interesting and useful discussion of African folklore and the reasons for its survival in the United States. In this discussion Bastide is careful to distinguish between black folklore and that which was created by whites for the purpose of making conversion to Christianity easier (pp. 179-184). Other topics covered by the author include the varying interpretations of Negritude here and in Africa, Africanisms in the Father Divine cult, and some general problems facing Afro-Americans in their attempts to identify with Africa.

In recent years there has been a proliferation of articles describing and evaluating African survivals in the New World. Those that deal with specific forms of survival such as music or art will be covered in the sections that follow. A good general introduction to the African origins of many aspects of American culture may be found in an article by Garrett (1966). Words like tote, tater, chimpanzee, etc., all stem from Africa. Dances such as the Mambo, Conga, Rhumba, and Charleston, were originally African. Different tales such as Uncle Remus and other animal stories have African roots. Black-eyed peas was the food originally eaten by the slaves during the Middle Passage from Africa, watermelon is still found growing wild in Africa, coffee comes from Kaffa, Ethiopia, and kola was originally an African drink. Although Garrett could also have made mention of Afro-American wood objects, pottery, and their African antecedents, his is a well-written and informative piece of work.

Slavery

An important link in establishing the continuity of African culture in the New World has been the slave experience. Thus a number of scholars have addressed themselves to the social and cultural structure of the African slave and the forms of African life that flourished within that community.

In his book From Sundown to Sunup: The Making of the Black
Community (1972), George P. Rawick describes how the American
slaves combined many African elements of their culture with
American ones. Much of this cultural synthesis was created
through the activities of the slaves at night after they had
finished the long day of work in the fields. Rawick emphasizes
that the reconstruction of their old world and the grafting of
it on to the new was essential of their survival. Relying heavily on excerpts from the slave interviews that were done in the
1930s by the Works Projects Administration, he presents a great
deal of material on the social, cultural, familial, and religious
lives of the slaves and demonstrates the extensive role played by
the African heritage in its development. From Sundown to Sunup
is actually the first of a nineteen-volume series. The other
eighteen volumes contain the actual slave narratives upon which
much of the material is based. For those interested in gaining
a full understanding of the slave experience and its connections
with African life this fascinating and authoritative book is indispensable.

Another excellent introduction to this topic is The Slave Community: Plantation Life in the Ante-Bellum South (1972) by John W.
Blassingame, which also deals with African survivals as they
appeared in slave culture. Blassingame points out (p. 2) that
the slaves were able to adjust to plantation life here because
many came from agrarian tribes such as the Ibo, Ewe, Wolof,
Bambara, etc. Of particular interest is the author's discussion
of music and dance forms that survived in various portions of the
United States, especially New Orleans.

In addition to the work of Rawick and Blassingame a number of
articles dealing with this topic have appeared in earlier years.
Highly recommended among these is a piece by Genovese (1960) that
evaluates the slaves' ability to work on the plantation in light
of their African heritage, and an article by Stuckey (1969) about
the African content in slave folksongs and tales.

Music and Art

In the area of general introductions to Africanisms in Afro-
American music a good starting point would be the first chapter
in Harold Courlander's Negro Folk Music, U.S.A. (1963).
Courlander stresses the importance of seeing Afro-American culture
as a mixture of European and African culture and takes the position that the musical abilities of black Americans are a result
of cultural rather than biological transmissions.

Perhaps the best discussions of black music in terms of African
survivals appears in Blues People (1963) by Imamu A. Baraka and
Urban Blues (1966) by Charles Keil. Baraka analyzes the historical development of Afro-American music in a perceptive and lucid
manner. According to him the sense of rhythm attributed to people
of African descent can be traced to the fact that African used

drums to communicate by phonetically reproducing the words, a
process that required great rhythmic sensitivity. In his discussion of religion in the black community Baraka gives a number
of reasons to account for the slaves' acceptance of Christianity.
Among these are the restrictions against the slaves' practicing
their own religion, the fact that the Africans always respected
the conquerors' Gods, and their awareness of the practical value
in adjusting to the white man's world (p. 32). Baraka also observes that Christianity, through its belief in heaven, took the
slaves' minds off the idea of returning to Africa (p. 39). Keil's
book is primarily about the structure, dynamics, and nature of the
world of jazz. In it Keil talks about interrelationships and
hybridization between European and African music: "West African
folk music and European folk music are enough alike to blend
easily in a seemingly infinite arrary of hybrids" (p. 30). Moreover, "in the blending process the African rhythmic foundation
absorbs and transforms the European elements." Keil does an excellent job of portraying the subtleties and complexities of jazz
music and of showing how its structure is capable of absorbing
within it a large variety of different types of music.

In an article dealing with similarities between West African and
Afro-American music Metcalfe (1970) finds at least two major point
points of comparison. The first is the social context of these
songs, i.e., the popularity of work songs in both cultures, and
the second is the similar tones, notes, verse forms, and call and
response patterns that are found in the music of both cultures.
Basically, however, this article is a review that presents very
little new materials and which relies heavily on quotes from other
sources. While Metcalfe begins by launching a general attack on
the research of white scholars in this area, saying: "No man has
the right to interpret another man's past," (p. 16) he later on
quotes from the work of quite a few whites, among them Herskovitz,
John, Keil, and others.

The work of Gunther Schuller is quite a bit more technical than
earlier works cited and is not recommended for readers with only
a casual interest in this subject. In his book Early Jazz: Its
Roots and Musical Development (1968), Schuller explains how the
African rhythms brought over by the slaves developed into early
jazz. Reading this book one gets a better appreciation of the
complexity of African music. In addition, the work demonstrates
how Afro-Americans actually simplified their music so as to allow
it to blend in with European influences and styles. For those
interested in obtaining hard facts concerning the African connections to Afro-American music Schuller's book is a must. Also of
value is a technical article by Lomax (1970) that attempts to
evaluate and compare Afro-American and African music by using
"cantometrics," a method of rating songs within the actual context
of their performance in order to discover and analyze their
characteristics. This approach differs from earlier ones that
evaluated printed versions of melodies or that examined the poetic
content of black and white spirituals (many of the earlier studies
had concluded, erroneously in Lomax's view, that the black spirituals were variants of white spirituals). Lomax's study concludes

that there are indeed a great number of similarities between
Afro-American and African music.

One of the best articles to appear on ths subject of similarities
in dance forms has been written by Cayou (1970) in which she
traces the development of black dance in America and compares
it to African dance forms. Cayou remarks that by trying to
eliminate expressions of African culture the plantation master
may actually have aided the development of new forms of expression
that were sufficiently divorced from African culture to emerge,
i.e., jazz, gospel, blues, etc. Cayou also makes the important
point that probably hundreds of cultural adaptations were lost
through the passage of time and because they were not seen and
subsequently institutionalized by the dominant white society.
Articles such as the one by Cayou go a long way towards demonstrating the resilience of black culture. Inasmuch as African dance
forms often expressed real-life situations, it is an indication of
the black community's vitality that it was able to take these
dance forms and successfully adapt them to the new lifestyles and
situations of the New World.

Writing in Blues People Baraka asserts that religion, music, and
dance retained a great deal of their African origins as opposed
to iron-working, wood-carving, and the like which "took a new
less obvious form or was wiped out altogether," (pp. 15-16). The
fact that someone as knowledgeable as Baraka could make this
assertion merely points up the value of Robert F. Thompson's
article on African art in the United States (1969). Thompson's
essay is a superb and valuable piece of work in an area that
has been all but ignored. In it he presents a great deal of
substantive material on the survival of many specific art forms
in the United States. In his discussion of various artifacts
produced in the United States by black craftsmen, such as wood-
carvings in New York and Georgia and stoneware in South Carolina,
Thompson traces the designs and motifs back to the specific
African tribes in which they originated.

Linguistics and Folklore

One of the more interesting articles to appear on the subject of
linguistics has been done by David Dalby (1972). Dalby gives
three reasons to explain why the contributions made by African
languages to English have gone unrecognized. One reason may have
been that so many languages are spoken in Africa that transfer-
ences may have occurred and gone unidentified. Second, the common
belief that black people lost their languages in the United
States, may have contributed to this unawareness. Finally, there
has been, according to Dalby, a lack of proper historical documentation in this area. Dalby maintains that English contains many
heretofore unnoticed words that are actually the result of English
and African words converging in addition to also having incorpo-
rated a number of expressions that were originally African. The
author presents a very useful list of 80 such words which he explains and traces back to their specific tribal origin. The importance of Dalby's article lies in the fact that it deals with

far more than the usual recitation of words that were directly
taken from African languages such as pinder, juju, goober, cooter,
etc., and presents new material in a refreshing style. Long
(1972) has also written a useful and informative article, though
it is somewhat more technical than Dalby's. Long talks about
the linguistic structure of African languages, particularly those
spoken in West Africa, and points out that despite the existence
of many different languages, the slaves were able to communicate
through the use of transactional dialects that were actually a
form of pidgin. Long also suggests that the linguistic peculiarities of many black Southerners such as substituting "d" and "t"
in place of "th" are based on the phonetics of West African
languages. We might add that while it is true that most languages
lack a "th" sound, the long survival of this substitution among
blacks as opposed to, say, French immigrants, is probably due
to the prolonged isolation of the black community that resulted
from slavery, segregation, and ghetto life.

A good introduction to the topic of Africanisms in New World folklore may be found in an article by Crowley (1962) that includes a
general discussion of the area and which takes note of some of
the problems involved in locating the origins of folktales.
Crowley talks about some of his own efforts to come to grips with
this problem in a later piece (1970) in which he gives an account
of a project he has initiated in this area. What he has done is
to gather over 12,000 tales from all over the world for the purpose of analyzing their content and origin through the use of a
type index and a motif index.[1] Vansertima (1971) has challenged
Crowley's assertion that many African tales originated in Europe.
Vansertima argues that such similarities as do exist may have
developed out of a common yet independent human experience and
that these similarities are coincidental rather than indicative
of cultural contact. His article also touches upon the geograph-
ical origins of Afro-Americans and attributes the proliferation
in this country of East African and Bantu tales to the fact that
while the slaves left from West Africa, many had come originally
from the Lower Congo. On the whole, this is an interesting and
thought-provoking article well worth reading.

Attitudes Toward Africa

With the upsurge of interest in Africa within the Afro-American
community a number of social scientists have turned their attention to the attitudes of Afro-Americans towards the African continent. These studies have been carried out in a wide range of
settings and exhibit a great deal of variation insofar as approach,
methodology, findings, and quality of work are concerned. Conse-
quently it would be premature at this stage to make general
statements and conclusions with regard to how Africa is perceived
in the black community. Many of these studies do, however,

---

[1] A type index numbers and documents tale types wherever they
have appeared and a motif index sets down incidents or characters
that occur repeatedly in various contexts.

provide insights and set the stage for future and more intensive
investigations.

Laosebikan (1972) reports on a study on the attitudes of Afro-
Americans toward Africa which employed the Social Distance Scale
developed by E.S. Bogardus. Using a sample of 100 Afro-Americans,
Laosebikan found that positive attitudes toward Africans ranked
second out of 30 ethnic groups surveyed. This was in contrast
to an earlier study (Goins and Meenes, 1960) that showed Africans
in fifth place behind the French, West Indians, Northern whites
in the United States, and Afro-Americans. Author suggests that
this change is due to the increased contact between Afro-Americans
and Africans and to the development of black consciousness in
recent years. On the whole, this article is somewhat superficial,
especially in its failure to discuss and evaluate the positioning
of the other 28 groups in the scale. Moreover, the author's
conclusion that blacks are more positively oriented toward Africa
in 1972 than they were ten or fifteen years ago is hardly surprising.

A good study has been done by Hoadley (1972) who compared the
views toward Africa of both whites and blacks in St. Louis. Based
on a questionnaire distributed to both groups Hoadley came up with
a number of interesting conclusions: Among blacks and whites who
evinced interest in Africa, blacks have more favorable attitudes
toward the continent. Young blacks were discovered to be in
favor of the United States government assuming a more active role
with regard to Africa to a greater extent that older blacks.
Whites were somewhat reluctant to have blacks "especially" consulted on matters pertaining to Africa and felt that both whites
and blacks should be asked to contribute their views. Based on
a content analysis of articles dealing with Africa, Hoadley found
that more articles on Africa appeared in white St. Louis newspapers than in black ones and concluded that, in general, blacks
are not more interested in Africa than are whites. The basis for
this conclusion can be questioned since black newspapers generally
(and certainly in St. Louis) represent primarily black middle-
class interests and are not good indicators of how the young and
the poor in the black community may feel. Thus while the author's
point may be valid, the evidence he presents is only applicable
to the black middle-class community. Going on the assumption
that white support for Africa is important in terms of general
government support for the continent, Hoadley concludes that the
general lack of white enthusiasm for Africa that emerged from his
study may indicate future difficulties for blacks who attempt to
influence United States foreign policy positively towards Africa.
While Hoadley's study would have been even more revealing had it
included a comparison of different socio-economic strata, the
material presented is informative and well-handled.

In late spring of 1969 Raymond H. Giles Jr. (1972) conducted a
study of the effects of an African heritage program that was
given in three Harlem elementary schools. The results raise
serious questions concerning the usefulness of such programs.
Giles discovered that many black Harlem schoolchildren were not

positively oriented toward Africa even after an intensive, nine-
month heritage program. The various classes sampled were taught
by three people with different backgrounds. One was an African
male, the second a white American male, and the third an Afro-
American female. As a result Giles questions whether pride can
be taught in the public school system as it is presently constituted. He suggests (but offers no proof) that the children's
attitudes were shaped by the dominant white culture long before
they entered school. One way of testing this assumption would be
to interview pre-school children and then interview them again
after they have been in school for a few years. Giles makes a
number of good suggestions for improving the awareness of children
in this area such as developing programs that concentrate on the
differences as well as on the similarities between African and
Afro-American culture and having teachers focus on dispelling
commonly-held stereotypes about Africa. This otherwise excellent
investigation could have been even better had it covered the
attitudes of the children before they began the heritage program.

A study done by Hicks and Beyer (1970) lends support to the
assertion made by many in the black community that the schools
have not (at least in the past) done a good job of teaching
students about Africa. In an investigation of attitudes of
secondary school students (seventh and twelfth graders) toward
Africa south of the Sahara it was found that while most students
knew something about Africa, they had many misconceptions about
the continent ranging from the belief that Timbuctu is most
famous for its diamonds (rather than universities) to the belief
that most of Africa is covered by jungles as opposed to grass-
lands. This despite the fact that most students have presumably
learned about Africa by the time they reach the twelfth grade.
In fact, a higher percentage of twelfth graders had incorrect
images about Africa than did seventh graders. The authors
criticize school programs for their superficiality and cite the
need for improving their content. The data for this study were
collected in 1967 and it is safe to assume that school programs
have, generally speaking, improved quite a bit since then.

A very interesting study (Krystall et al., 1970) has been made of
attitudes toward integration and black consciousness in a deep
South city. The data, which were gathered in 1967, concluded
that a substantial number of blacks favor both integration and
black consciousness and that the two positions were not mutually
exclusive. A total of 506 interviews were done, 240 of which
were with mothers or female guardians and 266 of which were with
high school seniors. Students were more likely to be interested
in visiting Africa, more likely to think of themselves as having
an African heritage, and more likely to be knowledgeable about
Africa although in general the level of knowledge was low compared
to the intensity of positive feelings about the continent. The
study also noted that African dress or hair style is a poor
indicator or separatist or integrationist views. Although many
middle-class blacks were proud of their African heritage they
were not as extreme in their views and were concerned as well with
successfully entering the mainstream of American society.

Another study of black students has been done by Wolkon (1971) who found that the Grade Point Average of students who identified with Africa was lower than that of students who did not.

Finally there are two studies of a more impressionistic nature that nevertheless offer some valuable insights into the conflicts facing black Americans in their efforts to develop a group identity. In his well-known book, The New World of Negro Americans, Harold R. Isaacs examined the views of 107 prominent Afro-Americans toward Africa and concluded that they had generally been ashamed of their background in the past. Considering the stereotypes of Africa that prevailed in the first half of the twentieth century, this result was not very surprising. More importantly, however, Isaacs concluded that his respondents were generally uninterested in Africa and, in some cases, rather disillusioned with their ancestral homes and that there was therefore no basis for the establishment of close ties between the two groups. Although the material presented in Isaac's book is highly interesting and stimulating, his methodological approach leaves much to be desired. The interviews he conducted were not systematic or representative of the black community as a whole. Rather they consisted of a "panel" of leaders who may well have been, because of their strategically located positions in the black community, far more cautious than the average person in expressing their true opinions on a matter as sensitive as this to a white interviewer. Another work by Inez S. Reid (1972) deals in part with the attitudes of black women toward Africa. Her interviews indicate a lack of knowledge about and interest in Africa on the part of many of her respondents. Although Reid's work contains many insights into this question it is more descriptive than analytical and barely touches upon the issue of why blacks do not relate to Africa.

When one considers the rate at which interest in and awareness of Africa has grown in recent years it becomes apparent that the studies discussed here must be viewed in terms of when they were carried out, for we are talking about a community that has undergone such tremendous changes in the past decade that a difference of two or three years can be very significant. We need, at this juncture, more studies of high quality to determine the future role of Africa in the Afro-American community. It is impossible to predict the future psychological importance of Africa in the black community or its cultural significance for these depend on too many factors, not the least important of which is how black people come to perceive their role and their opportunities in American society. Unforeseen political developments in Africa, especially South Africa, may also play a crucial role in the future involvement of Afro-Americans with the African continent. Economic opportunities or the lack of them may also exert an influence over many Afro-Americans as they attempt to carve out a satisfactory and productive environment for themselves and their families. Although the situation is sufficiently unclear at present to warrant projections into the future it is, nonetheless, clear that Africa is continuing to play a role of great importance in the black community and that because of its importance this is an area that deserves even greater attention than has been the case until now.

BIBLIOGRAPHY

Baldwin, J. Go Tell it on the Mountain, Dial, New York, 1963.

Bastide, R. African Civilizations in the New World, Harper & Row, New York, 1971.

Blassingame, J.W. The Slave Community: Plantation Life in the Ante-Bellum South, Oxford University Press, New York, 1972.

Bruchac, J. "Black Autobiography in Africa and America," Black Academy Review 2, pp. 61-70, Spring 1971.

Cayou, D.K. "The Origins of Modern Jazz Dance," Black Scholar 1, pp. 26-31, June 1970.

Cook, M. and S.E. Henderson. The Militant Black Writer in Africa and in the United States, University of Wisconsin Press, Madison, 1969.

Courlander, H. Negro Folk Music, U.S.A., Columbia University Press, New York, 1963.

Crowley, D.J., "Negro Folklore: An Africanist's View," Texas Quarterly 5, pp. 65-71, Autumn 1962.

Crowley, D.J. "African Folktales in Afro-America," in J.F. Szwed (ed.), Black America, Basic Books, New York, pp. 179-189, 1970.

Dalby, D. "The African Element in American English," in T. Kochman (ed.), Rappin' and Stylin' Out, University of Illinois Press, Urbana, pp. 170-186, 1972.

Ellison, R. Invisible Man, Random House, New York, 1947.

Garrett, R.B. "African Survivals in American Culture," Journal of Negro History 51, pp. 239-245, October 1966.

Genovese, E.D. "The Negro Laborer in Africa and in the Slave South," Phylon 21, pp. 343-350, Winter 1960.

Giles, R.H. Jr. Black and Ethnic Studies Programs at Public Schools: Elementary and Secondary, Center for International Education, School of Education, Amherst, Mass., pp. 29-57, 1972.

Goins, A.E. and M. Meenes, "Ethnic and Class Preferences Among College Negroes," Journal of Negro Education 29, pp. 128-133, Spring 1960.

Harlan, L.R. "Booker T. Washington and the White Man's Burden," American Historical Review 71, pp. 441-467, January 1966.

Herskovitz, M.J. The Myth of the Negro Past, Beacon Press, Boston, 1958.

_____. "The Ahistorical Approach to Afro-American Studies: A Critique," American Anthropologist 62, pp. 559-568, August 1960.

Hicks, E.P. and B.K. Beyer, "Images of Africa," Journal of Negro Education 39, pp. 158-166, Spring 1970.

Hoadley, J.S. "Black Americans and U.S. Policy Toward Africa," Journal of Black Studies 2, pp. 489-502, 1972.

Isaacs, H.R. The New World of Negro Americans, John Day, New York, 1963.

Jahn, J. Mantu: The New African Culture, Grove Press, New
   York, 1961.
Jones, L. (Imamu Amiri Baraka). Blues People, William Morrow
   and Company, New York, 1963.
Keil, C. Urban Blues, University of Chicago Press, Chicago,
   Ill., 1966.
Krystall, E.R., N. Friedman, G. Howze, and E.G. Epps. "Attitudes
   Toward Integration and Black Consciousness: Southern Negro
   High School Students and their Mothers," Phylon 31, pp. 104-
   113, Summer 1970.
Laosebikan, S. "Social Distance and Pan-Africanism," Afro-
   American Studies 3:3, pp. 223-225, 1972.
Lomax, A. "The Homogeneity of African - Afro-American Musical
   Style," in N.E. Whitten and J.F. Szwed (eds.), Afro-American
   Anthropology: Contemporary Perspectives, Free Press, New
   York, pp. 181-201, 1970.
Long, R.A. "From Africa to the New World: The Linguistic
   Continuum," in W.B. Abilla (ed.), Source Book in Black Studies,
   MSS Information Corporation, New York, pp. 37-45, 1972.
Metcalfe, R.H. Jr. "The Western African Roots of Afro-American
   Music," Black Scholar 8, pp. 16-25, June 1970.
Rawick, G.P. "The American Slave: A Composite Autobiography,"
   in From Sundown to Sunup: The Making of the Black Community,
   I, Greenwood Publishing Company, Westport, Conn., 1972.
Schuller, G. Early Jazz: Its Roots and Development, Oxford
   University Press, New York, 1968.
Stuckey, S. "Through the Prism of Folklore: The Black Ethos
   in Slavery," in J. Chametzky and S. Kaplan (eds.), Black and
   White in American Culture: An Anthology From the Massachusetts
   Review, University of Massachusetts Press, Amherst, pp. 172-
   191, 1969.
Thompson, R.F. "African Influence on the Art of the United
   States," in University, Yale University Press, New Haven,
   Conn., pp. 122-170, 1969.
Vansertima, I. "African Linguistic and Mythological Structures
   in the New World," in R.L. Goldstein (ed.), Black Life and
   Culture in the United States, Thomas Y. Crowell, New York,
   pp. 12-35, 1971.
Wolkon, G.A. "African Identity of the Negro American and
   Achievement," Journal of Social Issues 27:4, pp. 199-211, 1971.
Wright, R. Native Son, Harper & Brothers, New York, 1940.

AFRO-AMERICANS AND AFRICA

This bibliography has two broad purposes. First it is designed
to provide a handy reference for the interested scholar who
desires to know where research on the subject of Afro-Americans
and Africa may be found. It is especially intended for those
teaching in Afro-American studies programs around the country in
both colleges and secondary schools who wish to provide guidance
for their students in this area. Second, the bibliography provides a good starting point for the lay person unfamiliar with
the area in terms of where research on the subject may be found.
The subject index located at the end of the bibliography can direct the reader to specific topics.

Due to the dual purpose of this listing, both scholarly and non-
scholarly articles and books have been included. The period
covered, 1960-1973, was chosen because its years fall into the
era of Black history, often referred to these days as the Second
Reconstruction, a time when the Black community's interest in
Africa and Black nationalism in general reached new, perhaps
unparalleled heights. Despite this interest, efforts to organize
the available material on this subject have been minimal, hence
the justification for compiling this list of almost 400 titles.
Many of these titles have been annotated and a good number contain
critical comments in addition to summarizing their contents. The
criteria used in determining which works would be commented on
were the quality of the work, its representativeness, and/or
freshness of the material. The writer accepts responsibility for
what is, unavoidably, a somewhat arbitrary decision. Although
an effort was made to list everything published on the topic
there are surely works that have not come to the author's attention. It is hoped that further research in the area will fill in
some of these gaps. In some cases only a section of an article
or book deals with Africa and in such instances we have indicated
that this is the case. The terms Afro-American, Black, Black
American, and American Black have been used interchangeably,
largely for the sake of not being too repetitious in style. Finally it is hoped that awareness of the amount of work done on
this subject will stimulate others to do more research in what is
one of the most crucial chapters in the Black experience in the
United States.

GENERAL BIBLIOGRAPHY OF WORKS
ON AFRO-AMERICANS AND AFRICANS

General Works

Akiwowo, A. "Racialism and Shifts in the Mental Orientation of
Black People in West Africa and in the Americas, 1856 to
1956", Phylon 31, Fall (1970) pp. 256-264.

Bell, H.H. "Negro Nationalism: A Factor in Emigration Projects
1858-1861", Journal of Negro History 47, January (1962)
pp. 42-53.

Bracey, J., A. Meier, and E. Rudwick (eds.), Black Nationalism in
America, (Indianapolis: Bobbs-Merrill, 1970) especially
pp. 38-48, pp. 77-86, pp. 114-120, pp. 156-210.

Davis, J.A. (ed.), Africa Seen by American Negro Scholars, (New
York: American Society of African Culture, 1963).

Drake, S.C. "Negro Americans and the Africa Interest" in J.P.
Davis (ed.), The American Negro Reference Book, (Englewood
Cliffs, N.J.: Prentice-Hall, 1966) pp. 662-705.

Draper, T. The Rediscovery of Black Nationalism, (New York:
Viking, 1969).

James, C.L.R. A History of Pan-African Revolt, (Washington, D.C.:
Drum and Spear Press, 1969, 2nd ed. rev.).

Kilson, M. and A.C. Hill (eds.), Apropos of Africa: Afro-American Leaders and the Romance of Africa, (New York: Anchor,
1971).

Shepperson, G. "Notes on Negro American Influences on the Emergence of African Nationalism", Journal of African History,
1, 2 (1960) pp. 299-312.

Shepperson, G. "Pan-Africanism: Some Historical Notes", Phylon
23, Winter (1962) pp. 346-358.

Shepperson, G. "The African Diaspora --- Or the African Abroad",
African Forum 2, 1 (1966) pp. 76-93.

Skinner, E.P. Afro-Americans and Africa: The Continuing Dialectic, (New York: The Trustees of Columbia University, 1973)
Pamphlet.

Stuckey, S. The Ideological Origins of Black Nationalism,
(Boston: Beacon Press, 1972).

Uya, O.E. (ed.), Black Brotherhood: Afro-Americans and Africa,
(Lexington, Mass.: D.C. Heath, 1971).

Slavery

Blassingame, J.W. The Slave Community: Plantation Life in the
Ante-Bellum South, (New York: Oxford University Press, 1972)
pp. 1-40.

Genovese, E.D. "The Negro Laborer in Africa and in the Slave
South", Phylon 21, Winter (1960) pp. 343-350.

Levine, L. "Slave Songs and Slave Consciousness: An Exploration
in Neglected Sources", pp. 99-126 in T.K. Hareven (ed.),
Anonymous Americans: Explorations in Nineteenth Century
Social History, (Englewood Cliffs, N.J.: Prentice-Hall,
1971).

Rawick, G.P., The American Slave: A Composite Autobiography.
Vol. 1; From Sundown to Sunup: The Making of the Black
Community, (Westport, Conn.: Greenwood Publishers, 1972).

Reed, H.A. "Slavery in Ashanti and Colonial South Carolina",
Black World 20, February (1971) p. 37.

Stuckey, S. "Through the Prism of Folklore: The Black Ethos of
    Slavery", pp. 172-191 in J. Chametzky and S. Kaplan (eds.).
    Black and White in American Culture: An Anthology From the
    Massachusetts Review, (Amherst: University of Massachusetts,
    1969).
Stuckey, S. "Slave Resistance as Seen Through Slave Folklore",
    pp. 51-60 in I.S. Reid (ed.), Black Prism: Perspectives on
    the Black Experience, (New York: Faculty Press, 1969).

Religion
Coan, J.R. The Expansions of Missions of the A.M.E. Church in
    South Africa, 1896-1908, (Hartford, Connecticut: Hartford
    Seminary, 1961), Ph.D. Dissertation.
Drake, S.C. The Redemption of Africa and Black Religion, (Chica-
    go: Third World Press, 1970).
Epps, A. "A Negro Separatistist Movement of the Nineteenth Cen-
    tury", Harvard Review, 4, Summer (1969) pp. 69-87.

American Colonization Society
Redkey, E. Black Exodus: Black Nationalism and Back to Africa
    Movements 1890-1910, (New Haven: Yale University Press,
    1969).
Staudenraus, P.J. The African Colonization Movement, 1816-1865,
    (New York: Columbia University Press, 1961).

Negro Convention Movement
Bell, H.H. (ed.) Minutes of the Proceedings of the National Negro
    Conventions 1830-1864, (New York: Arno Press, 1969).
Pease, W.H. and J.H. Pease. "The Negro Convention Movement", in
    N.I. Huggins, M. Kilson, and D.M. Fox (eds.), Key Issues in
    the Afro-American Experience (Vol. 1), (New York: Harcourt,
    Brace, Jovanovich Inc., 1971) pp. 191-205.

Liberia and Sierra Leone
Akpan, M.B. The African Policy of the Liberian Settlers 1841-
    1932: A Study of the Native Policy of a Non-Colonial Power
    in Africa, (Ibadan, Nigeria: University of Ibadan, 1968),
    Ph.D. Dissertation.
Akpan, M.B. "Liberia and the Universal Negro Improvement Associa-
    tion: The Background to the Abortion of Garvey's Scheme for
    African Colonization", Journal of African History, 14, 1
    (1973) pp. 105-127.
Balfit, S. "American-Liberian Relations in the Nineteenth Centu-
    ry", Journal of Human Relations, 10, Summer (1962) pp. 405-
    418.
Chalk, F. "Du Bois and Garvey Confront Liberia: Two Incidents
    of the Coolidge Years", Canadian Journal of African Studies,
    1, 2 (1967) pp. 135-141.
Fyfe, C. A History of Sierra Leone, (London: Oxford University
    Press, 1962).
Hargreaves, J.D. "African Colonization in the Nineteenth Century
    ---Liberia and Sierra Leone", pp. 55-76 in J. Butler (ed.),
    Boston University Papers in African History, Vol. 1, (Boston:
    Boston University Press, 1964).
Harris, S.H. "An American's Impressions of Sierra Leone in 1811",
    Journal of Negro History, 47, January (1962) pp. 35-41

3

Jones, H.A.B. The Struggle for Political and Cultural Unifica-
tion in Liberia, 1847-1930, (Evanston, Illinois: North-
western University, 1962), Ph.D. Dissertation.
Harris, S.H. Paul Cuffe: Black America and the African Return,
(New York: Simon and Schuster, 1972).
West, R. Back to Africa: A History of Sierra Leone and Liberia,
(London, 1970).

Martin R. Delaney
Bell, H.H. "Introduction", in M.R. Delaney and R. Campbell,
Search For a Place: Black Separatism and Africa, 1860,
(Ann Arbor: University of Michigan Press, 1969), pp. 1-22.
Kirk-Greene, A.H.M. "America in the Niger Valley: A Colonization
Centenary", Phylon, 23, Fall (1962) pp. 225-239.
Sterling, D. The Making of an Afro-American: Martin Robison
Delaney, 1812-1885, (New York: Doubleday, 1971).
Ullman, V. Martin R. Delaney: The Beginnings of Black National-
ism, (Boston: Beacon Press, 1971).

Alexander Crummell
Scruggs, O.M. We the Children of Africa in the Land: Alexander
Crummell, (Washington, D.C.: Howard University, 1972),
Ph.D. Dissertation.
Wahle, K.O. "Alexander Crummell: Black Evangelist and Pan-Negro
Patriot", Phylon, 29, 4 (1968) pp. 388-395.

Edward Wilmot Blyden
Billingsley, A. "Edward Blyden: Apostle of Darkness", Black
Scholar, 2, December (1970) pp. 3-12.
Henriksen, T.H. "Edward W. Blyden: His Influence on Contemporary
Afro-Americans", Pan-African Journal, 4, Summer (1971)
pp. 255-265.
Holden, E. Blyden of Liberia: An Account of the Life and Labor
of Edward Wilmot Blyden, L.L.D., as Recorded in Letters and
in Print (New York: Vantage Press, 1966).
Jones, W.D., "Blyden, Gladstone, and the War", Journal of Negro
History, 49, January (1964) pp. 56-61.
Lynch, H.R. "Edward Wilmot Blyden: Pioneer West African Nation-
alist", Journal of African History, 6, 3 (1965) pp. 373-388.
Lynch, H.R. Edward Wilmot Blyden: Pan-Negro Patriot, 1832-1912,
(New York: Oxford University Press, 1967).

Henry M. Turner
Redkey, E.S. "Bishop Turner's African Dream", Journal of Ameri-
can History, 54, 2 (1967) pp. 271-290.
Redkey, E.S. Black Exodus: Black Nationalist and Back to Africa
Movements, 1890-1910, (New Haven: Yale University Press,
1969).
Redkey, E.S. "The Flowering of Black Nationalism: Henry McNeal
Turner and Marcus Garvey", in N.I. Huggins, M. Kilson, and
D. Fox (eds.) Key Issues in the Afro-American Experience
(Vol. 2), (New York: Harcourt, Brace, Jovanovich Inc.,
1971), pp. 107-124.

Booker T. Washington
Harlan, L.R. "Booker T. Washington and the White Man's Burden",
    American Historical Review, 71, January (1966) pp. 441-467.
Mabata, J.C. "Booker T. Washington and John Tengo Jabavu: A
    Comparison", Afro-American Studies, 2, 3 (1971) pp. 181-186.

Alfred Charles Sam
Bittle, W.E. and G.L. Geis. "Alfred Charles Sam and an African
    Return: A Case Study in Negro Despair", Phylon, 23, June
    (1962) pp. 178-194.

Ethiopia
Contee, C.G. "Ethiopia and the Pan-African Movement Before 1945",
    Black World, 21, February (1972) p. 41.
Ross, R. "Black Americans and Italo-Ethiopian Relief", Ethiopian
    Observer, 15, 2 (1972) pp. 122-131.
Weisbord, R.G. "Black America and the Italian Ethiopian Crisis:
    An Episode in Pan-Negroism", The Historian, 34, 2 (1972)
    pp. 230-241.

W.E.B. Du Bois
Aptheker, H. "Du Bois on Africa and World Peace: An Unpublished
    Essay", Political Affairs, 47, February (1968) pp. 81-89.
Blair, T.L. "Du Bois and the Century of African Liberation",
    pp. 8-14 in A. Berrian and R. Long (eds.), Negritude: Essays
    and Studies, (Hampton, Virginia: Hampton Institute Press,
    1967).
Chalk, F. "Du Bois and Garvey Confront Liberia: Two Incidents
    of the Coolidge Years", Canadian Journal of African Studies,
    1, 2 (1967) p. 135.
Clarke, J.H., E. Jackson, E. Kaiser, and J.H. O'Dell (eds.) Black
    Titan: W.E.B. Du Bois, (Boston: Beacon Press, 1970).
Contee, C.G. "The Emergence of Du Bois as an African National-
    ist", Journal of Negro History, 54, January (1969) pp. 48-63.
Du Bois, S.G. His Day is Marching On, (Philadelphia: Lippincott,
    1971), especially pp. 298-378.
Du Bois, W.E.B. "Ghana Calls", Freedomways, 2, Winter (1962)
    pp. 71-74.
Fonlon, B. "The Passing of a Great African", Freedomways 5,
    Winter (1965) pp. 195-206.
Hansberry, W.L. "W.E.B. Du Bois' Influence on African History",
    Freedomways, 5, Winter (1965) pp. 73-87.
Isaacs, H.R. "Du Bois and Africa", Race, 2, November (1960)
    pp. 3-23.
Lacy, L.A. The Life of W.E.B. Du Bois: Cheer the Lonesome Trav-
    eler, (New York: Dial Press, 1970).
Moore, R.B. "Du Bois and Pan-Africa", Freedomways, 5, Winter
    (1965) pp. 166-187.
Paschal, A.G. "The Spirit of W.E.B. Du Bois" (Part I), Black
    Scholar, 2, October (1970) pp. 17-28.
Paschal, A.G. "The Spirit of W.E.B. Du Bois" (Part II), Black
    Scholar, 2, February (1971) pp. 38-50.
Walden, D. and K. Wylie. "W.E.B. Du Bois: Pan Africanism's
    Intellectual Father," Journal of Human Relations, 14,
    1 (1966) pp. 28-41.

5

Marcus Garvey

Akpan, M.B. "Liberia and the Universal Negro Improvement Associa-
     tion: The Background to the Abortion cf Garvey's Scheme for
     African Colonization", Journal of African History, 14, 1
     (1973) pp. 105-127.
Bennett, L. "The Ghost of Marcus Garvey", Ebony, 15, March
     (1961) pp. 53-61.
Chalk, F. "Du Bois and Garvey Confront Liberia: Two Incidents
     of the Coolidge Years", Canadian Journal of African Studies,
     1, 2 (1967) pp. 135-141.
Edwards, A. Marcus Garvey, 1887-1940, (London and Port-of-Spain:
     Beacon Publications, 1967).
Elkins, W.F. "The Influence of Marcus Garvey on Africa: A
     British Report of 1922", Science and Society, 32, Summer
     (1968) pp. 321-323.
Essien-Udom, E.U. "Introduction", in Philosophy and Opinions of
     Marcus Garvey, (London: Frank Cass Ltd., 1967) 2nd ed.,
     2 v.
Fax, E. Garvey: The Story of a Pioneer Black Nationalist, (New
     York: Dodd, Mead, and Co., 1972).
Garvey, A.J. Garvey and Garveyism, (Kingston, Jamaica, 1963).
Garvey, A.J. The Philosophy and Opinions of Marcus Garvey,
     (London: Frank Cass Ltd., 1967). 2nd ed., 2 v.
Garvey, A.J. "Marcus Mosiah Garvey", Negro Digest, 18, May (1969)
     p. 42.
Garvey, A.J. "Garvey and Pan-Africanism: A Wife's Footnote to
     Black History", Black World, 21, December (1971) pp. 15-18.
Hart, R. "The Life and Resurrection of Marcus Garvey", Race, 9,
     2 (1967) pp. 217-237.
Langley, J.A. "Marcus Garvey and African Nationalism", Race, 10,
     2 (1969) pp. 157-172.
Moses, W. "Marcus Garvey: A Reappraisal", Black Scholar, 4,
     November-December (1972) pp. 38-49.
Redkey, E.S. "The Flowering of Black Nationalism: Henry McNeal
     Turner and Marcus Garvey", in N.I. Huggins, M. Kilson, and
     D.M. Fox (eds.), Key Issues in the Afro-American Experience,
     (New York: Harcourt, Brace, Jovanovich Inc., 1971), Vol. 2,
     pp. 107-124.
Sundiata, T. "A Portrait of Marcus Garvey", Black Scholar, 2,
     September (1970) pp. 7-19.
Vincent, T.G. Black Power and the Garvey Movement, (Berkeley:
     Ramparts Press, 1970).

Malcolm X

Clarke, J.H. (ed.). Malcolm X: The Man and His Times, (New York:
     Collier's, 1969).
Epps, A. "The Theme of Exile in Malcolm X's Harvard Speeches",
     The Harvard Journal of Negro Affairs, 2, 1 (1968) pp. 40-
     54.
Goldman, P. The Death and Life of Malcolm X, (New York: Harper
     & Row, 1973).
X, Malcolm (with the assistance of A. Haley). The Autobiography
     of Malcolm X, (New York: Grove Press, 1965), especially
     pp. 343-363.

Miscellaneous

Hooker, J.R. "The Negro American Press and Africa in the Nine-
    teen Thirties", Canadian Journal of African Studies, 1,
    March (1967) pp. 43-50.
King, K.J. "Africa and the Southern States of the U.S.A.: Notes
    on J.H. Oldham and American Negro Education for Africans".
    Journal of African History, 10, 4 (1969) pp. 659-677.
Shaloff, S. "William Henry Sheppard: Congo Pioneer", African
    Forum, 3, 4 (1968) pp. 51-62.
Stuckey, S. "The Cultural Philosophu of Paul Robeson", Freedom-
    ways, 11, 1 (1971) pp. 78-90.

AFRO-AMERICANS AND AFRICA:
A SELECTED BIBLIOGRAPHY

AHMED, MUHAMMED (Max Stanford). "The Roots of the Pan-African Revolution." In: Black Scholar, San Francisco, Calif., May 1972, pp. 48-55. Consists primarily of a summation of the various positions vis-a-vis Africa taken in recent years by different segments of the Afro-American community. Discussing those who favor closer ties with Africa, Ahmed says that although it is important to help "the brothers and sisters on the mainland" (p. 52), Black people should direct their efforts towards the struggle in the United States since this is where they are colonized. Talks about the need for a world-wide Black revolution if Africa is to become truly free. Does not advance any specific proposals on how such unification might be achieved saying: "A revolutionary never warns the world of what he is going to do. He does it." (pp. 49-50)   (1)

AIKINS, LENTON. "Pan-Africanism: Self Determination and Nation Building." In: Black World, Chicago, November 1971, p. 23. (2)

AKAR, JOHN J. "Is Black Beautiful to Africans?" In: New York Times, New York, October 31, 1970, p. 29:1. A popularly written article by Sierra Leone's Ambassador to the United States. Points out that Africans were always convinced that Black is beautiful but that the opposite idea that white is therefore ugly does not necessarily follow. Since Africans must deal with the white world (they are poor), they simply cannot afford to alienate the white world. Expresses the hope that Black Americans will achieve greater equality in their country and that this will result in their being able to lobby more effectively for African interests.   (3)

AKIWOWO, AKINSOLA. "Racialism and Shifts in the Mental Orientation of Black People in West Africa and the Americas, 1856 to 1956." In: Phylon, Atlanta, Ga., Fall 1970, pp. 256-264.   (4)

AKPAN, M.B. The African Policy of the Liberian Settlers 1841-1932: A Study of the Native Policy of a Non-Colonial Power in Africa. Ibadan, University of Ibadan, 1968, 1.   (5)

AKPAN, M.B. "Liberia and the Universal Negro Improvement Association: The Background to the Abortion of Garvey's Scheme for African Colonization." In: Journal of African History, New York, Vol. 14, No. 1, 1973, pp. 105-127. Excellent, well-documented account of Marcus Garvey's plan to settle Black Americans in Liberia with special emphasis upon the reasons for Liberia's negative response to those plans. Akpan argues that Liberia was afraid of alienating certain European powers in Africa, especially France and England, and that she was apprehensive that the presence of a Garveyite group in Liberia might compel the ruling class there to cease its exploitation of the native population.   (6)

ALBERT, ALAN. "A Study in Brown." In: Albert Berrian and Richard Long (eds.), Negritude: Essays and Studies, Hampton, Va., Hampton Institute Press, 1967, pp. 79-88. (7)

ALLEN, ROBERT L. Black Awakening in Capitalist America, New York, Doubleday, 1969, 25 pp. (8)

ALLEN, SAMUEL W. "Negritude and its Relevance to the American Negro Writer." In: American Society of African Culture (ed.), The American Negro Writer and His Roots, New York, American Society of African Culture, 1960, pp. 8-20. Discussion of Negritude and the importance of the African heritage to the Afro-American. Says that while the Afro-American will, in the long run, be more concerned with his American heritage, Africa is still of crucial significance. Allen argues that the Black American has lost a good deal of his African culture and points out that while Africans were also enslaved in the past they were at least in their own home and constituted a majority. Even the West Indian was in the majority throughout most of his history and had less contact with whites than his North American counterpart. Allen asserts that an understanding of the African heritage assumes even greater importance when one considers that in the United States, Africa itself is the source of many distortions and caricatures about Black people. (9)

_____. "Negritude: Agreement and Disagreement." In: American Society of African Culture (ed.), Pan-Africanism Reconsidered, Berkeley, University of California Press, 1962, pp. 310-323. (10)

_____. "The African Heritage." In: Black World, Chicago, January 1971, pp. 14-18. (11)

AMERICAN SOCIETY OF AFRICAN CULTURE. Constitution of the American Society of African Culture, 1959. (available at the Schomburg Library, New York). The purpose of this organization, namely, to examine the effect of African culture upon American life and to eliminate biases that limit such an appreciation, is explained in its constitution. Among its activities were the giving of books to African countries, holding conferences, trips to Africa, and the like. (12)

_____. "An American Writer in Africa." In: Negro Digest, Chicago, December 1962, pp. 41-48. (13)

_____. Annual Report, 1959-1960. (available at the Schomburg Library, New York). (14)

_____. Annual Report, 1964-1965. (available at the Schomburg Library, New York). (15)

_____. Proposed Program, 1960-1961. (available at the Schomburg Library, New York). (16)

9

ANDERSON, S.E. "Revolutionary Black Nationalism and the Pan-African Idea." In: Floyd Barbour (ed.), The Black Seventies, Boston, Porter-Sargent, 1970, pp. 99-126. An examination of the future goals of the Black Movement. Concludes that such goals should be political in their orientation. Discussing Africa, the author concludes that African culture needs a "political framework." As for Afro-Americans, they must develop a perspective that lies in their struggle with that of the exploited peoples of Africa and those of the Third World on other continents as well. This approach is necessary because of the global nature of white racism and imperialsim. Due to their interest in the struggle for human rights and justice, Africans and Afro-Americans share common goals and bonds. A good portion of this article focuses upon matters of interest to the Black community not directly related to Africa.   (17)

_____. "Revolutionary Black Nationalism is Pan-Africanism." In: Black Scholar, San Francisco, Calif., March 1971, pp. 16-22.   (18)

APTHEKER, HERBERT. "Du Bois on Africa and World Peace: An Unpublished Essay." In: Political Affairs, New York, February 1968, pp. 81-89.   (19)

BALDWIN, JAMES. "A Negro Assays the Negro Mood." In: New York Times, New York, March 12, 1961, section 6:25. Baldwin argues that while the Afro-American's home is the United States, he is nevertheless, greatly affected by seeing independence come to various African nations and them comparing it to the discrimination against Blacks that exists in the United States. Baldwin asserts that the pro-Lumumba demonstration at the United Nations was indicative of general Black discontent throughout the world. Rather brief an somewhat superficial, but well written.   (20)

_____. The Fire Next Time, New York, Dial Press, 1962, 120 pp.   (21)

BALFIT, SINGH. "American-Liberian Relations in the 19th Century." In: Journal of Human Relations, Wilberforce, Ohio, Summer 1962, pp. 405-418.   (22)

BARAKA, IMAMU AMIRI. Beginning of National Movement, Newark, Jihad Production, 1972, pamphlet.   (23)

_____. "The Pan-African Party and the Black Nation." In: Black Scholar, San Francisco, Calif., March 1971, pp. 24-32.   (24)

_____. Strategy and Tactics of a Pan-African Nationalist Party, Newark, National Involvement CFUN, 1971, pamphlet.   (25)

_____. "Toward the Creation of Political Institutions for all African Peoples." In: Black World, Chicago, October 1972,

pp. 54-78. Discussion of the 1972 Black Political Convention held in Gary, Indiana, Baraka feels that Afro-Americans
should work for an Africa that is not only strong and unified
but which will also reward such efforts on its behalf with
support for Afro-American interests.   (26)

_____. ed. African Congress: A Documentary of the First
Modern Pan-African Congress. New York, William Morrow and
Company, 1972. 493 pp. This is a record of speeches given
and the proceedings of workshops held at the Congress of
African Peoples which took place in September 1970 in Atlanta,
Georgia. Among the most important presentations for our
topic is one by the Reverend Jesse Jackson which argues that
the development of love and respect for Black people everywhere is far more important than the wearing of dashikis,
learning about ancient Africa, or visiting the continent.
Accoreing to Jackson, Africans will respect this position.

Richard Hatcher in his speech regards cultural differences
as a barrier to repatriation for Afro-Americans. At the
same time he sees Africa as important in terms of developing
psychological security.

Baraka also feels emigration to be unrealistic, largely
because most Black people are not interested in the idea.
He says it is important to develop a base of power around
Africa in order to win respect for Black people everywhere.
On the one hand Baraka talks about how it is essential that
Afro-Americans become "a functional ally to African and Third
World peoples" (p. 108) (emphasis added). At the same time
he offers the view that the real unity of Black people finds
its roots in Blackness. Where than does this leave non-Black,
Third World groups? Perhaps Baraka is saying that these
groups are important but not as important in terms of the
needs of Black people. The underlying theme of Baraka's position as expressed in the book is a willingness to work together; "We will form alliances with Third World peoples who
show a willingness to support our goals and aims." (p.169).

Ayuko Babu suggests that Blacks become involved with Tanzania, Zambia, and Guinea because these nations have been most
active in supporting liberation movements throughout the
African continent. Other relevant statements are by Howard
Fuller and Hannibal El-Mustafa Ahmed. Among the resolutions
passed at the Congress were that money be raised for the
building of the Tanzanian-Zambian railroad, that combat boots
be sent to African liberation forces, and the establishment
of a "Black international development bank."

This is one of the most important books on the topic to appear
in the last decade. In addition to indicating the many ways
in which Blacks have perceived Africa, it demonstrates the
militant approach toward Africa that is being taken in the
1970s as opposed to the more moderate stance adopted by the
American Society of African Culture during the early sixties.

Above all, one notes the cultural and historical emphasis
of the **articles** that appeared in the book edited by AMSAC
in 1958 and the political emphasis of the present work. The
decidedly African thrust of the Congress may be seen from its
name, the fact that Black Americans are repeatedly referred
to as Africans, the number of African speakers, the resolutions passed, and, of course, the discussions themselves.
Moreover, Baraka states in his introduction that the Congress
is in the tradition of the Pan-African meetings initiated by
W.E.B. Du Bois.

Because of a common history of white oppression and due to
an increased awareness among Black Americans of its depth,
it is clear that African liberation efforts, especially in
South Africa and Rhodesia, have become and will continue to
be **an** important rallying point in the Afro-American community.
Such interest is likely to be even greater should the United
States decide to actively defend South Africa and Rhodesia
in their attempts to perpetuate white domination and control.
This work is basic reading for those interested in the
subject.   (27)

BARRETT, LINDSAY. "Should Black Americans Be Involved in African
    Affairs?" In: Negro Digest, Chicago, August 1969, pp. 10–
    17.   (28)

BASTIDE, ROGER. African Civilizations in the New World. New
    York, Harper & Row, 1971, especially pp. 162–226. Translated
    from the French, this is an important work concerning African
    and Afro-American culture in the New World, especially with
    respect to religion. The author makes a number of incisive
    and interesting points with respect to the United States.

Although many patterns of behavior are unique to Black Americans, Bastide asserts that they are affected by a mentality
that still retains African ways of thinking, i.e. the desire
for group association. While Blacks have borrowed from white
American revivalism (which originated in Scotland) in their
religious behavior, there are some important differences
between the two. For example, the whites have onlookers and
performers, the Blacks performers only. Also, among the
whites movements are rather disorganized and jerky whereas
among the Blacks they are more rhythmic and coordinated. In
the final analysis, however, Bastide concludes, both patterns
influenced each other.

Bastide discusses the Father Divine Cult (pp. 163–64) and its
relationship to African culture. In his discussion of African culture, Bastide gives several important reasons to account
for its survival in the United States, albeit in somewhat
different form. First, the masters understood that allowing
the slaves to practice their own customs was essential for
their mental health. Second, they hoped that the dances, many
of which were erotic, would result in greater sexual activity
among the slaves that would in turn produce more slaves. Third,

12

from the Black perspective, folktales, especially where the
weak emerged victorious over the powerful, were important for
the slaves in view of their oppressed condition. Finally,
the Europeans, finding many of the tales enjoyable, published
a good number of them, thereby ensuring their preservation
(p. 172). Significantly, the author distinguishes between
Black folklore and that created by whites for the purpose of
making conversion to Christianity a smoother process.

Bastide notes that, generally speaking, New World Africans,
in their reidentification with Africa have been unwilling to
push matters to their "logical end", namely polytheism and
animism (p. 217), and argues that this is partly because they
have absorbed the white view that such beliefs are a lot of
nonsense. While the author actually makes this point with
respect to the Black Muslims it can be said to apply to
Christianity as well, neither of which originated in Black
Africa.   (29)

BELL, HOWARD H. "Introduction" In: Martin R. Delaney and
   Robert Campbell, Search for a Place: Black Separatism and
   Africa, 1860. Ann Arbor, University of Michigan Press, 1969,
   pp. 1-22.   (30)

_____. "Negro Nationalism: A Factor in Emigration Projects
   1858-1861." In: Journal of Negro History, Washington, D.C.,
   January 1962, pp. 42-53. An interesting article that evaluates
   sentiment favoring Black emigration from the United States,
   especially to Haiti, during the 1858-61 period. Author discusses the view of various Black leaders of that time, particularly Martin Delaney and Frederick Douglass and shows the
   shifts made by the latter in his position on the emigration
   issue. Bell speculates that emigration sentiment would have
   received a far more favorable reception had it not been for
   the Civil War, Douglass would have been a very strong supporter
   of emigration as a solution to the problems facing Afro-
   Americans.   (31)

BENNETT, LERONE, JR. "The Ghost of Marcus Garvey." In: Ebony,
   Chicago, March 1960, pp. 53-61. Interviews about Garvey's
   life with his two former wives, Amy Ashwood and Amy Jacques.
   Concerning Africa, Ms. Ashwood said: "Although he was not
   the first to visualize a strong and independent Africa, he
   gave the idea the new urgency and a tremendous impetus."
   (p. 58). Ms. Jacques was quoted as follows on this question:
   "The term back-to-Africa was used and promoted by newspapers,
   Negro newspapers mostly, to ridicule Garvey. There was no
   back-to-Africa movement except in a spiritual sense. But
   migration was planned to Liberia because concessions were
   given there. The idea was to take only enough to establish
   a township as an example and pattern for Africans. He never
   advocated mass migration. The idea is ridiculous." (pp. 59-
   60). We might add that as with Malcolm X, the Reverend Martin
   Luther King, and others, it is difficult to assess how Garvey
   would have reacted vis-a-vis Africa had his career not been

cut short by circumstances beyond his control.   (32)

_____. "What's in a Name? Negro vs. Afro-American vs. Black."
In: Ebony, Chicago, November 1967, pp. 46-54.   (33)

BERRY, FAITH. "On Richard Wright in Exile: Portrait of a
Man As Outsider." In: Negro Digest, Chicago, December
1968, pp. 26-37.   (34)

BILLINGSLEY, ANDREW. "Edward Blyden: Apostle of Blackness."
In: Black Scholar, San Francisco, Calif., December 1970,
pp. 3-12.   (35)

BITTLE, WILLIAM E. AND GILBERT L. GEIS. "Alfred Charles Sam
and an African Return: A Case Study in Negro Despair." In:
Phylon, Atlanta, Ga., June 1962, pp. 178-194.   (36)

_____. The Longest Way Home. Detroit, Wayne State University
Press, 1964, 229 pp. The account of an attempt in 1914 by
Chief Alfred Charles Sam of Oklahoma to lead sixty Afro-
Americans back to Africa on a boat which eventually sailed
for the Gold Coast. Although Sam stayed, the mission was
unsuccessful, as most found life there too difficult and returned to the United States. Book relies largely upon news-
paper accounts and is somewhat lacking in its failure to
provide a serious analysis of this event. It is, however,
a highly readable work and raises the possibility that
similar movements may have existed but were unrecorded simply
because they never got off the ground.   (37)

BLAIR, THOMAS L. "Du Bois and the Century of African Liberation." In: Albert Berrian and Richard Long (eds.), Negritude: Essays and Studies. Hampton, Va., Hampton Institute
Press, 1967, pp. 8-14.   (38)

BLASSINGAME, JOHN W. The Slave Community: Plantation Life
in the Ante-Bellum South, New York, Oxford University Press,
1972. 262 pp., especially pp. 1-40. Deals with African
survivals as they appeared in slave culture as part of a
more general discussion of religion, music, dance, language
forms, and folktales. Points out that the slaves were able
to adjust to life here in part because they came from
agrarian tribes such as the Ibo, Ewe, Wolof, Bambara, etc.,
(p. 2). Of particular interest is the discussion of music
and dance forms that survived in the New Orleans area. An
excellent introduction to the whole topic.   (39)

BLAUNER, ROBERT. Racial Oppression in America. New York,
Harper & Row, 1972, 309 pp., especially pp. 124-
161. Blauner presents a forceful argument for the uniqueness
of Afro-American culture. Points out that, unlike other
groups, Blacks did not follow the immigrate-assimilate process.
If anything, it is the reverse, although in reality, Blacks
have tended to alternate between the identity of the immigrant
and that of the assimilationist. Notes that "Black"

14

refers to ethnicity as much as it does to color. Argues that
we may have failed to clearly perceive the influence of Africa
on Black culture because we looked for it in the wrong place.
Rather than searching for it in its material and behavioral
aspects we should look to the spiritual side i.e. soul-negri-
tude and the philosophy of African culture. While Blauner's
criticism of the emphasis placed by scholars may be valid, it
must be noted that soul and spirit are difficult things to
capture. In fact, if they were "captured" they might no
longer be spirit or soul! By definition and of necessity
perhaps, such parts of a people's culture are elusive in terms
of their being analyzed and evaluated.   (40)

BOND, HORACE M. "Howe and Isaacs in the Bush: The Ram in the
    Thicket." In: Negro History Bulletin, Washington, D.C.,
    December 1961. A strongly worded attack on articles written
    by Harold Isaacs and Russell Howe in which they asserted that
    Afro-Americans and Africans do not like each other. Bond
    cites personal experiences that he had in Africa which prove
    the opposite and criticizes the methodology used by Isaacs in
    arriving at his conclusions. He also discusses the history
    of the relationships between the two groups in order to show
    that they have had extensive and fruitful contact through the
    years.   (41)

BORDERS, WILLIAM. "U.S. Blacks Visiting Africa Find that the
    Feeling of Kinship is Not Always Shared." In: New York Times,
    New York, September 5, 1971, p. 23.   (42)

BOURGUIGNON, ERIKA E. "Afro-American Religions: Traditions
    and Transformations." In: John F. Szwed (ed.), Black Ameri-
    ca, New York, Basic Books, 1970, pp. 190-202. Most of this
    article focuses upon African survivals in the Catholic portions
    of the New World. Writer repeats the oft-stated thesis that
    there were more survivals there than in areas under Protestant
    influence because Catholicism was more receptive to the Afri-
    can view of the world as one in which there many gods existed.
    In her comments on the United States, Bourguignon points to
    certain forms of worship in fundamentalist and pentecostal
    churches noting the African nature of the rhythms and the anti-
    phonal exchange of chanting between leader and chorus. This
    entire area is deserving of further investigation -- namely,
    to what extent did the white churches develop these practices
    on their own or import them from Europe and to what degree did
    they incorporate them from the patterns followed in the Afro-
    American community?   (43)

BRACEY, JOHN, AUGUST MEIER AND ELLIOTT RUDWICK (eds.). Black
    Nationalism in America. Indianapolis, Bobbs-Merrill, 1970.
    568 pp., especially pp. 38-48; 77-86; 114-120; 156-210.   (44)

BRAITHWAITE, E.R. A Kind of Homecoming. Englewood Cliffs,
    N.J., Prentice-Hall, 1962, 243 pp. Personal account of
    experiences while visiting Africa in 1961 by a native of
    British Guiana who also lived in New York City for a number

of years. Rather sketchy and impressionistic.   (45)

BROWNE, ROBERT S. "The Case for Black Separatism." In:
Ramparts, Berkeley, Calif., December 1967, pp. 46-51. Argues
for the establishment of a separate Black homeland within the
United States. Says that while some Afro-Americans may have
found a home in Africa, for the majority the separation from
the continent has been too long in terms of cultural loss
thus making them (Afro-Americans) feel like strangers in Africa. Besides, asserts Browne, Blacks have shed a great deal
of blood and sweat in the United States thus justifying a
homeland here. Does not specify where such a homeland should
be located.   (46)

_____ AND JOHN H. CLARKE. "The American Negro's Impact." In:
Africa Today, Denver, Col., January 1967, pp. 16-18. Laments
the lack of attention given Africa by the majority of Black
Americans. Gives a very short history of such involvement
and the accomplishments generated by it. Also cites the
integrationist ethic as a barrier towards the development in
this country of identification with Africa.   (47)

_____, HOLLIS LYNCH AND MAJOR WRIGHT. "Three Writers on the
Question of Repatriation." In: Freedomways, New York, Summer
1968, pp. 255-261. Robert Browne argues that those Blacks in
the United States who need economic help the most are un-
skilled for the most part, and are therefore least likely to
be wanted in Africa. Urges more serious consideration of
partition in the United States. Hollis Lynch is generally
supportive of the idea of repatriation but cautions that it
is valid only for a portion of the Afro-American population
(which portion he does not say) and that it should therefore be seen as complementary to other programs. Suggests
the United Nations or the Organization of African States as
organizations capable of coordinating such a plan. Major
Wright takes the position that the real enemy, Western
Imperialism, is operative in Africa as much as it is in Harlem
or Watts. Moreover, if skilled Blacks were to emigrate they
would drain the brain-power of the Black community in this
country. Repatriation, in Major's view, should be primarily
for political refugees who are committed to the Struggle so
that they do not have to stagnate in Canada or Europe. Argues
that a great deal depends on whether one goes to a progressive
African land or to one dominated by Imperialist or pro-Imperial-
ist interests.   (48)

BRUCHAC, JOSEPH. "Black Autobiography in Africa and America."
In: Black Academy Review, Buffalo, New York, Spring 1971,
pp. 61-70. Interesting article comparing various autobiograph-
ical works by Afro-American and African writers with an aim of
demonstrating similarities among certain writers of both groups.
Some of the authors paired off in this manner are Booker T.
Washington and Kwame Nkrumah and Chief Albert Luthuli; Prince
Modupe and Claude Brown; Richard Wright and Camara Laye.
Although the idea is intriguing Bruchac should after noting

the autobiographical nature of these works, have attempted to explain why this form of writing developed as a response to the condition of Black people. For example, why not more novels instead that deal with people in the third person? If, on the other hand, the writer believes that he has only chosen one of many possible art forms that could be compared in this manner he should state so explicitly.   (49)

CARMICHAEL, STOKELY. Stokely Speaks: Black Power Back to Pan-Africanism. New York, Vintage Books, 1971, 229 pp., especially pp. 145-227. Collection of speeches in which Carmichael discusses his experiences while living in Africa and why Afro-Americans should support it. Says Africa is the true home of all Black people and that it will give American Blacks a strong base of support if it is a strong continent.   (50)

_____. "We are All Africans." In: Black Scholar, San Francisco, Calif., May 1970, pp. 15-19. Text of a message sent from Guinea to Malcolm X Liberation University on the occasion of its opening dedication ceremony. In it, Carmichael asserts that all Black people in the world are really Africans due not only to their origins but also because of the nature of white oppression. Author urges Blacks to go to Africa and help in its development. Article does not even touch upon some of the cultural differences that may exist between Afro-Americans and Africans. Though such differences may not be all that important, they should at least be mentioned. Looking to the future, another question needs to be raised: If large numbers of educated and talented Afro-Americans emigrate to Africa, might they one day be perceived as an American elite blocking the aspirations of upwardly mobile Africans educated and brought up in Africa? Clearly this would depend, among other things, on how well they integrate themselves into African life and culture, but in any event it is a topic in need of further discussion.   (51)

CARTEY, WILFRED. "Current Themes in African and Afro-American Literature." In: Inez Smith Reid (ed.), The Black Prism: Perspectives on the Black Experience, New York, Faculty Press, 1969, pp. 119-124.   (52)

CAYOU, DOLORES K. "The Origins of Modern Jazz Dance." In: Black Scholar, San Francisco, Calif., June 1970, pp. 26-31. Traces the history of the development of Black dance in the United States and compares it to African dance forms. A fine article in which the author makes a number of interesting observations: First, the master may even have encouraged the development of new forms of dance that appeared sufficiently divorced from Africa such as gospel, blues, spirituals, etc. simply through his overt efforts to stamp out expressions of African culture. Also, there were probably hundreds of cultural adaptations that were lost to us largely because they were not seen by whites and therefore institutionalized (though many have come to us via the slave narratives done in the 1930s). Articles such as this go a long way towards demon-

strating the resilience of Black culture. Inasmuch as African dance forms often expressed real-life situations, it is
an indication of the vitality and creativeness of Black people that they were able to take these dance forms and adapt
them to different lifestyles and new situations.   (53)

CHALK, FRANK. "Du Bois and Garvey Confront Liberia: Two Incidents of the Coolidge Years." In: Canadian Journal of African Studies, Ottawa, Vol. 1, No. 2, 1967, pp. 135-141.   (54)

CHAPMAN, ABRAHAM. "The Black Aesthetic and the African Continuum." In: Pan-African Journal, Nairobi, Fall 1971, pp. 397-
406.   (55)

CHASE, JUDITH W. Afro-American Art and Craft. New York, Van
Nostrand, 1971, 142 pp.   (56)

CHICK, C.A. "The American Negro's Changing Attitude Toward
Africa." In: Journal of Negro Education, Washington, D.C.,
Fall 1962, pp. 531-535. Author points out that although Afro-
Americans have not shown as great an interest in Africa as
other American groups have evinced toward their lands of
origin, this is changing and for several reasons: a. A
better understanding of African history and its contributions
to the world b. More knowledge about the achievements of
the early arrivals to the New World c. Greater personal
contact between members of the two groups in colleges and
various programs. Unfortunately, Chick, in this rather
superficial article, does not explain in any depth how and
why this interest began to develop in the early 1960s. It
is no doubt true, as Chick says, that more people are now
reading the works of men such as Carter Woodson, but the
question is --- why? Chick should have tied his observations
into the Black Movement of the sixties, which by 1962, was
well underway and ought also to have mentioned the emergence
of independent African states that was occurring at the time
in more and more portions of the continent.   (57)

CLARK, JOHN P. America, their America. London, Heineman, 1964,
221 pp. This is primarily an account by an African of his
experiences in America. For our purposes it contains a
critique of the American Society of African Culture as an
elitist organization. Clark also levels a general criticism
against Afro-Americans who adopt external symbols of Africa
without a real understanding of their meaning.   (58)

CLARKE, JOHN H. "Africa and the American Negro Press." In:
Journal of Negro Education, Washington, D.C., Winter 1961,
pp. 64-68.   (59)

_____. "African Studies in the United States: An Afro-Ameri-
can View." In: Africa Today, Denver, Col., April-May, 1969,
pp. 10-12. Attacks the lack of attention given, in the past,
to the contributions of Black scholars such as Lorraine
Hansberry, Joel A. Rogers, Arthur Schomburg, and others.

Blames domination by whites of the field for this situation. Chides American Society of African Culture and the African Studies Association for not focusing enough on Afro-Americans and Africa in their programs. Also takes the view that there is a need to concentrate more on the pre-colonial period in African history. (60)

_____. "Afro-American Search." In: Pan-African Journal, Nairobi, Fall 1968, pp. 182-183. (61)

_____. "Black Power and Black History." In: Negro Digest, Chicago, February 1969, pp. 35-44. (62)

_____. "The Fight to Reclaim African History." In: Negro Digest, Chicago, February 1970, p. 10. (63)

_____. "The Growth of Racism in the West." In: Black World, Chicago, October 1970, pp. 4-10. (64)

_____. "The Impact of the African On the New World ----- A Reappraisal." In: Black Scholar, San Francisco, Cal., February 1973, pp. 32-39. (65)

_____. "The Neglected Dimensions of the Harlem Renaissance." In: Black World, Chicago, November 1970, pp. 118-129. (66)

_____. "The New Afro-American Nationalism." In: Freedomways, New York, Fall 1961, pp. 285-295. Basically an explanatory and descriptive article in which the author talks about the then emerging Black nationalism and pride, particularly interest in Africa. Emphasizes that Afro-Americans and Africans are both trying to establish their identity by synthesizing the best of African culture ie. the communal socialism of the past with modern-day needs and imperatives. Afro-Americans, argues Clarke, are discovering anew the importance of using history and culture to develop unity and self-respect. Article also contains a brief description of various Afro-American nationalist groups including the New Alajo Party and the Cultural Association for Women of African Heritage. (67)

_____. "Reclaiming the Lost African Heritage." In: American Society of African Culture (ed.), The American Negro Writer and his Roots, New York, American Society of African Culture, 1960, pp. 21-27. (68)

_____. (ed.) Malcolm X: The Man and his Times. New York, Colliers, 1969, 360 pp. Twenty-nine selections dealing with Malcolm X. Includes interviews, interpretive essays, speeches, etc. Also contains a statement outlining the goals and objectives of Malcolm X' Organization of Afro-American Unity. A very important book inasmuch as Malcolm X was very much involved in forging links between Afro-Americans and Africans. For individual selections from the book that appear in bibliography see Index under Politics and Ideology. (69)

_____, ESTHER JACKSON, ERNEST KAISER, AND J.H. O'DELL (eds.).
Black Titan: W.E.B. Du Bois. Boston, Beacon Press, 1970,
333 pp.   (70)

CLEAVER, ELDRIDGE. "Culture and Revolution: Their Synthesis
in Africa." In: Black Scholar, San Francisco, Cal., Vol. 3,
No. 2, 1971, pp. 33-39.   (71)

_____. "The Land Question and Liberation." In: Ramparts,
Berkeley, Cal., May 1968, pp. 51-53. Points out that Black
people, like any other group, have always hungered for land.
Arguing that Black people in this country are already a nation,
Cleaver states that they ought to begin "functioning as a
nation" and should demand a plebiscite supervised by the United
Nations for America's Black ghettoes. While recognizing that
the creation of such a plebiscite would be highly unlikely,
Cleaver believes that demands of this sort will internationa-
lize the problem and create a crisis for capitalist America.
Does not discuss the feasibility of emigration to Africa as
an alternative beyond noting that Marcus Garvey was unable to
implement his program of resettlement in Africa.   (72)

CLENDENEN, CLARENCE, ROBERT COLLINS, AND PETER DUIGNAN. Americans in Africa, 1865-1900. Stanford, Cal., Hoover Institution,
1966, 130 pp. This volume deals with Americans in Africa,
trade between the two continents, relations with Liberia,
explorations in Africa, American involvement in Zanzibar and
South Africa, and other, related topics. Focuses more upon
general history and only tangentially with the role of Afro-
Americans.   (73)

_____. Americans in Black Africa Up to 1865. Stanford, Cal.,
Hoover Institution, 1964, 109 pp. An important document evaluating the role played by Afro-Americans and whites in Africa.
Combines missionary reports, government dispatches, and personal accounts.   (74)

COAN, JOSEPHUS R. The Expansion of Missions of the A.M.E.
Church in South Africa, 1896-1908. Hartford, Conn., Hartford
Seminary, 1961.   (75)

COBB, CHARLIE. "Africa Notebook: Views on Returning Home."
In: Black World, Chicago, May 1972, pp. 22-37.   (76)

COHEN, DE SILVER. "The Vindictive and non-Vindictive Aspects
of Black Literature: The Anti-Colonialism Theme." In:
Black Lines, Pittsburgh, Pa., Vol. 1, No. 1, 1970, pp. 40-
45.   (77)

COHEN, ROBERT D. "African Students and the Negro American:
Past Relationships and a Recent Program." In: International
Educational and Cultural Exchange, Washington, D.C., Vol. 5,
No. 2, 1969, pp. 76-85.   (78)

COLEMAN, BEVERLY. "A History of Swahili." In: <u>Black Scholar</u>, San Francisco, Cal., February 1971, pp. 13-25. (79)

_____. "Relevancy in Teaching and Learning About Swahili." In: <u>Black World</u>, Chicago, October 1970, pp. 11-24. A factual discussion of Swahili, its structure, and uses, and why Black people should study it. Includes an annotated bibliography of works on Swahili. (80)

COLLINS, LEONARD E. JR. "The Afro-American Return to Africa in the Twentieth Century --- Illusion and Reality." In: <u>Afro-American Studies</u>, New York, Vol. 3, No. 2, pp. 103-109. Excellent introduction to the subject of expatriation among Afro-Americans to Africa. After a brief historical introduction, the author turns his attention to more recent times, beginning with the reactions of Richard Wright and James Baldwin to expatriation, continues with the views of lesser-known, yet similarly motivated Blacks, and ends with a brief discussion of Afro-Americans in Ghana and their experiences there both before and after Nkrumah's downfall. Collins pays particular attention to the expectations of emigrating Black Americans and to the problems they face in integrating with African society and culture. (81)

CONTEE, CLARENCE G. "Afro-Americans and Early Pan-Africanism." In: <u>Negro Digest</u>, Chicago, February 1970, pp. 24-30. (82)

_____. "The Emergence of Du Bois as an African Nationalist." In: <u>Journal of Negro History</u>, Washington, D.C., January 1969, pp. 48-63. Scholarly review and analysis of W.E.B. Du Bois' development as a Pan-Africanist with particular emphasis on his participation in the First Pan-African Conference held in London in July 1900. (83)

_____. "Ethiopia and the Pan-African Movement Before 1945." In: <u>Black World</u>, Chicago, February 1972, p. 41. (84)

COOK, ANN. "Black Pride? Some Contradictions." In: <u>Negro Digest</u>, Chicago, January 1970, p. 36. (85)

COOK, MERCER AND STEPHEN E. HENDERSON. <u>The Militant Black Writer in Africa and in the United States</u>. Madison, Wis., University of Wisconsin Press, 1969, 136 pp. This interesting little book does a good job of showing some of the historical, cultural, and literary parallels in the experiences of Afro-Americans and Africans. Soul, Negritude, music, and poetry, are among the many topics touched upon. (86)

COURLANDER, HAROLD. <u>Negro Folk Music, U.S.A.</u>. New York, Columbia University Press, 1963. 324 pp., especially pp. 1-14. General work dealing with Black folk music. For our topic the first chapter is important. It consists of a useful, though not terribly extensive, review of African survivals in Afro-American culture. Courlander observes that musical abilities of Black people, wherever they appear,

are the result of a transmittal of cultural heritage rather
than biological traits. Points out that hair styles such
as plaiting designs were common in the South many years ago
and are common in Haiti and in the West Indies (for those
who assume the cornrow to be a new development).   (87)

COVINGTON, JUANITA ANN. "My Experiences in Ethiopia." In:
Crisis, New York, March 1964, pp. 147-152.   (88)

"Crisis in African Studies." In: Africa Today, Denver, Col.,
October-November-December 1969, pp. 1-31, Almost the entire
issue is devoted to a discussion by various scholars, Black
and white, of the African Studies Association Annual Meeting
held in Montreal in 1969. The Meeting was highlighted by
certain demands made by the African Heritage Studies Association. Among the demands were: racial parity on Association
committees. Association was accused of excluding Blacks
(both Africans and Afro-Americans) from positions of power
within the organization.   (89)

CROWLEY, DANIEL J. "African Folktales in Afro-America." In:
John F. Szwed (ed.), Black America, New York, Basic Books,
1970, pp. 79-189. Author, an anthropologist, discusses
a project that he has initiated in which he has gathered over
12,000 folktales from all over the world. Crowley intends
to analyze these tales by constructing a type index (this
numbers and documents "tale types" wherever they have appeared)
and a motif index (which sets down incidents or character
that appear repeatedly in various contexts and among different cultures). One of the major goals of the study will be
to discover the origin of African folktales.   (90)

_____. "Negro Folklore: An Africanist's View." In: Texas
Quarterly, Austin, Texas, Autumn 1962, pp. 65-71. Primarily
an evaluation of the work done by Melville J. Herskovitz and
Richard M. Dorson as it relates to Africanisms in New World
folklore. Also dwells on some of the problems in locating
the origins of folktales. Notes that while there exist many
retentions in the United States, it has least amount among
those parts of the New World where they may be found.   (91)

CRUSE, HAROLD W. "Revolutionary Nationalism and the Afro-
American." In: Studies on the Left, New York, Vol. 2,
No. 3, 1962, pp. 12-25.   (92)

_____. The Crisis of the Negro Intellectual. New York, William
Morrow and Co., 1967, 594 pp., especially pp. 420-448. While
acknowledging the potential of the group he refers to as the
"Afro-American nationalists" should they ever become unified,
Cruse is highly critical of them. Among other things, he
charges them with an inability to unite or form a political
party, of leaving the leadership of the Black community to the
integrationists, of rejecting bourgeois help because it is
bourgeois when they are themselves, in many instances, of
bourgeois origins. He also attacks their views as romantic

and unrealistic particularly because they try to deny any
influence upon them of American culture. Cruse also warns
that taking the Blackness and African identifications too
far could result in an ideology of Black supremacy. A
good part of this discussion is also devoted to an examination
of relations between Afro-Americans and West Indians. This
is strong stuff coming as it does from a Black nationalist
who is well known in the Black and white community. Whether
one agrees or disagrees with Cruse, his views are presented
in an interesting and challenging manner.   (93)

CUDJOE, SELWYN R. "Criticism and the Neo-African Writer."
In: Black World, Chicago, December 1971, pp. 36-48.   (94)

DALBY, DAVID. "The African Element in American English."
In: Thomas Kochman (ed.), Rappin' and Stylin' Out, Urbana,
Ill., University of Illinois Press, 1972, pp. 170-186. An
important article about linguistic survivals in the English
language. Author gives three reasons to explain why people
have failed to recognize the contributions to English made
by African languages: a. There are so many different
languages spoken in Africa; b. The prevalent belief that
Blacks lost their languages as a result of slavery; c. The
lack of proper historical documentation. Dalby argues that
there are many heretofore unnoticed words whose origins lie
in African languages. These are often either the result of
English and African words converging or actual African expressions that were translated into English. An example of the
latter would be "day-clean" which is the term in Mandingo
for dawn. Author presents a list of eighty such words which
he not only explains bur traces back to the specific tribes
among whom they originated. The list is particularly useful because the list includes far more than the usual lists
of well-known words such as cooter, goober, pinder, juju,
etc..   (95)

_____. Black Through White: Patterns of Communication.
Bloomington, Indiana, African Studies Program.   (96)

DAVIS, JOHN A. "Black Americans and United States Policy
Toward Africa." In: Journal of International Affairs,
Montpelier, Vermont, Capital City Press, Vol. 23, No. 2,
1969, pp. 236-249. General article in which author talks
about AMSAC, the American Negro Leadership Conference, the
rise of Black nationalism, and related topics. Remarks
(p. 148) that in the near future Black nationalists will
be representing the interests of the Afro-American in
Africa. While deploring the potential divisiveness of this
in terms of how it will affect American policy toward Africa, Davis sees hope in the fact that many more Black people
are studying about Africa in universities and in the rise of
Black urban politicians who, he feels, will eventually take
control of the Black nationalist movement.   (97)

_____. (ed.). Africa Seen by American Negro Scholars. New

York, American Society of African Culture (Second Printing), 1963, 418 pp. Originally published as a special edition by the French journal Presence Africaine. Contains numerous excellent essays by prominent scholars. First two portions of the book deal with African society while the third part assesses various aspects of the relationships of Afro-Americans with Africa. Among the articles most relevant to our topic is "Traditional NAACP interest in Africa (as reflected in the pages of the Crisis)," (pp. 229-246) which talks about the role of the NAACP and the Crisis in advancing knowledge and understanding about the African continent. Written by James Ivy, it is a solid piece of work. Horace Mann Bond's article "Forming African Youth: A Philosophy of Education" (pp. 247-262), is a historical discussion of role played by Lincoln Univeristy in educating African youths. "The American Negro's View of Africa." (pp. 217-228), by Rayford Logan, is a very brief and general discussion of Black attitudes toward Africa from the turn of the Twentieth Century. E. Franklin Frazier's article "What Can the American Negro Contribute to the Social Development of Africa," (pp. 263-278), concludes that, for the most part, Blacks can contribute very little to Africa. More than anything else, Frazier's reasons (they have no political power, have an inferior education, and lack technical skills) reveal how much the position of Afro-Americans has changed in the last decade. Despite this, the article is valuable for the historical perspective it gives us. The collection also contains articles by W.E.B. Du Bois (first published in 1933) and John A. Davis about Liberia. Adelaide Hill contributes an article titled "African Studies Programs in the U.S.," (pp. 361-378) which discusses how and why such programs have developed. Specific programs are evaluated. This is followed by a 421-item bibliography on Afro-Americans and Africa compiled by Dorothy B. Porter and covering the period 1788-1958. Though it is not annotated, it is, nonetheless, a very valuable tool for scholars interested in this area. Finally there is a piece about the Journal of Negro History's contribution to interest in Africa by Ulysses Lee. Perhaps the greatest usefulness of this book is as a historical backdrop to the recent resurgence of scholarly and general interest in Africa during the 1960s.   (98)

DELANEY, PAUL. "Carmichael Back in U.S. Seeks Black Unity." In: New York Times, New York, November 14, 1972, p. 22:1. (99)

"Dialogues with Africans: African-American Institute and Other Conferences." In: New York Amsterdam News, New York, March 27, 1971, p. 15.   (100)

DRAKE, ST. CLAIR. "The American Negro's Relation to Africa." In: Africa Today, Denver, Col., December 1967, pp. 12-15. Concise outline of the history of Afro-American involvement in Africa from 1619-1966. Contains a useful "fact sheet" enumerating the more important developments. Drake defends the role of the Black church in Africa, arguing that it was sincere and adopted an "Africa for the Africans" position. Urges Afro-American support for Africa because, among other things, "we are all in the same boat." (101)

_____. "'Hide my Face?' On Pan-Africanism and Negritude." In: Herbert Hill (ed.), Soon One Morning, New York, Alfred A. Knopf, 1963, pp. 78-105. Excellent discussion of attitudes toward Africa in the Twentieth Century. Evaluates concept of Negritude, cultural and political Pan-Africanism, and the effects these ideas and movements have had and are likely to have on the Black community. While acknowledging that the influence of Africa on Black people will depend, in the final analysis, on the individual, Drake seems to feel that its greatest impact will be on the psychological needs of Black Americans to take pride in their history and identity. Drake says that while "Africa will probably welcome the few exiles" who leave the United States "there will not be any compaigns urging them to "come home"". Considering that this article was written in 1963 it was remarkably accurate in predicting the current increase of interest in Africa. (102)

_____. "Negro Americans and the Africa Interest." In: John P. Davis (ed.), The American Negro Reference Book, Englewood Cliffs, New Jersey, Prentice-Hall, 1966, pp. 662-705. Fine summary of African-Afro-American relations from the 19th Century to the mid-1960s. (103)

_____. "The Negro's Stake in Africa." In: Negro Digest, Chicago, June 1964, pp. 33-48. (104)

_____. The Redemption of Africa and Black Religion. Chicago, Third World Press, 1970, 80 pp. Discussion of the history of Black religion in America with particular emphasis on the contacts with Africa by various Black leaders. Also dwells on how African culture developed in America. One of the most interesting parts of the book is an evaluation of the role played by Ethiopia in Black religious and nationalist thought. Drake also looks at what happened when African and Christian concepts of religion came into contact with each other. (105)

DRAPER, THEODORE. "The Fantasy of Black Nationalism." In: Commentary, New York, September 1969, pp. 27-54. A critical review article covering the history of Black nationalism in America. Attacks the idea of applying the colonization model to Afro-Americans because Blacks here are not on their own soil. Furthermore, Draper asserts that "A true colony aims at more than full participation" (p. 41). Rather it seeks to overthrow the powers that be. Discusses the attitudes of the Black Panthers and the cultural nationalists such as Harold Cruse and Imamu Amiri Baraka with special emphasis on their position regarding the "land question." While one can easily quibble with Draper's view that a colonized minority needs to be on its own land to be so considered, this is a useful piece whose importance lies in its portrayal of the varieties of Black nationalism. The views of Julius

25

Lester, Eldridge Cleaver, and Floyd McKissick are just a few
of those touched upon and the ideologies evaluated include
Black capitalism, revolutionary socialism, and the position
adopted by the Republic of New Africa.   (106)

_____. The Rediscovery of Black Nationalism. New York,
Viking Press, 1969. 211 pp.   (107)

DU BOIS, DAVID G. "Afro-American Militants in Africa." In:
Black World, Chicago, 1972, February 1972, pp. 4-11.   (108)

_____. "The Souls of Black Folk." (Part I). In: The Black
Panther, San Francisco, Calif., September 30, 1972, p. 2.
Rather short article in which the author, who lived in Africa
for thirteen years talks about himself and his stepfather,
W.E.B. Du Bois. States that he himself lived there because
he felt welcome and at ease in Africa. Emphasizes that his
stepfather did not leave the United States because of any
ideological contradictions but because Nkrumah had invited
him to live in Ghana while working on the Encyclopedia Afri-
cana. Moreover, he points out that Du Bois never gave up
his American citizenship. He simply became a Ghanaian citi-
zen as well.   (109)

_____. "The Souls of Black Folk." (Part II). In: The Black
Panther, San Francisco, Calif., January 6, 1973, p. 2. A
continuation of the first article to appear in this journal.
Du Bois describes how he had to learn not to think of himself
only in terms of being Black. In sum, these articles leave
a good deal unsaid. One gets the feeling that only a superficial effort has been made. Surely Du Bois could have said
more after spending thirteen years in Africa.   (110)

DU BOIS, SHIRLEY GRAHAM. His Day is Marching On. Philadelphia,
Pa., J.B. Lippincott, 1971, 384 pp. especially pp. 298-378.
Last portion of this biography is a personal account of Du
Bois' final years which he spent in Africa. While interesting,
it does not deal with the father of Pan-Africanism's views
on Afro-Americans and their relationships with Africa. Yet,
the account is important in terms of seeing how one of history's greatest Black leaders reacted to Africa and what his
experiences were. In considering the relative paucity of
information on how Du Bois perceived the relationship between Blacks the world and Africa one must remember certain
factors. First Du Bois' own involvement with Africa, in a
sense, speaks for itself. Second, he died in 1963 before
Afro-American consciousness of Africa reached its apex in
the sixties. Third, Du Bois was as much a Pan-Africanist
in terms of the African continent as he was an advocate of
closer ties between Black Americans and Africans and that
the latter was only one of many interests that this remark-
able individual had.   (111)

DU BOIS, W.E.B. "Ghana Calls." In: Freedomways, New York,
Winter 1962, pp. 71-74.   (112)

26

DUNBAR, ERNEST. "The Black Revolt Hits the White Campus."
In: Look, New York, October 31, 1967, pp. 27-31.   (113)

_____. (ed.) The Black Expatriates. New York, Pocket
Books edition, 1970, 221 pp. Essays by Afro-Americans who
left the U.S. for Africa and Europe. In looking at the
various pieces on Africa we find a good deal of diversity
among the viewpoints presented. Gloria Lindsey talks about
her experiences in Tanzania and Kenya, shedding light on
what it is like to be an Afro-American woman in Africa.
Tom Feelings, an activist who lived in Ghana, discusses his
need to leave this country in order to discover whether or
not his art was being evaluated on the basis of his color.
Priscilla Stevens Kruize's story is somewhat different.
She married a white Dutchman, came to Ghana to live, and
discovered, among other things, that she had more in common
with Europeans and white Americans than with black Ghanaians.
Dr. Robert E. Lee is a Black dentist who came to Africa
(Ghana) for idealistic reasons. He attributes his successful adjustment to having made a real effort to integrate
himself fully into African society and culture, particularly
learning the language. One of the best articles is by Bill
Sutherland, a pacifist who has worked for the Ghanaian and
Tanzanian governments and who makes some very perceptive
observations. He came to Africa because he felt disillusioned, not only with racism, but also with the type of society
American represented in general. Although he feels that
African goals and values may be going in the same direction
he believes that Africa is still, at this stage, a newer
and more fluid society. Sutherland points out some difficulties that arriving Blacks may face: 1. The movement in
Africa is more of a continental than a racial one as was
the case prior to independence. 2. Africans are suspicious
of Afro-Americans because of Liberia's treatment of its
native population. 3. There exists some bad will because
of the exploitive activities of some Afro-Americans in the
past. 4. A Fear that Afro-Americans might someday be a
fifth column in their midst. Despite these problems,
author believes that Afro-Americans can be accepted in Africa provided they are patient, understanding, and realistic.
Sutherland distinguishes between those Blacks who leave
the United States because they have rejected American society and those who depart because they really wanted to be
accepted by it but feel they have not been. These essays,
which are actually interviews, are full of insights into
how Blacks respond to and feel about everyday life and
problems in Africa. Must reading for anyone thinking about
making a trip to Africa who wants to find out more about the
subject. It may be added that, though they are not germane
to this topic, the essays dealing with Europe are also well
worth reading.   (114)

DUNDES, ALAN. "African Tales Among the North American Indians."
In: Southern Folklore Quarterly, Gainesville, Fla., September

1965, pp. 207-219.   (115)

ECHEWA, THOMAS O. "Africans vs. Afro-Americans." In: Negro
Digest, Chicago, Ill., January 1965, pp. 33-38.   (116)

_____. "Reply to an American Negro." In: Negro Digest,
Chicago, Ill., September 1965, pp. 23-27.   (117)

EDMONDSON, LOCKSLEY. "Black Power: A View From the Outside."
In: Africa Today, Denver, Col., December 1967, pp. 6-9.
Jamaican author assesses the relevance of the Black power
theme for Blacks in the Caribbean and in Africa. He evaluates
the political, psychological, and economic aspects of Black
power for the United States, Africa, and the Caribbean and
concludes, among other things, that the psychological aspect,
with its emphasis upon pride, is the most significant of all
three. The political form is judged problematical in the
United States by Edmondson because Blacks there have no
territorial base and are a numerical minority. Also their
situation is not as desperate as, say, that of Black South
Africans. Edmondson considers economic considerations more
relevant than political ones in the United States but not
as realizable in that country as elsewhere, largely because,
in his opinion, Blacks here lack political power.   (118)

_____. "Race and Human Rights in International Organization
and International Law -- and Afro-American Interests:
Analysis and Documentation." In: Afro-American Studies,
New York, December 1971, pp. 205-217. Discussion of how
Afro-Americans can fight racism. Author suggests that one
way of doing this would be through becoming involved in the
United Nations-sponsored International Convention on the
Elimination of All Forms of Racial Discrimination. While
admitting that this group is not very influential in terms
of present accomplishments, Edmondson feels involvement is
important for the purpose of internationalizing the struggle
against racism and colonialism. Takes note of African
support of the Afro-American struggle against racism as
seen by the Organization of African States' proclamation
regarding slavery, colonialism, and racism made in 1971.   (119)

EDWARDS, ADOLPH. Marcus Garvey, 1887-1940. London and Port-
of Spain, Beacon Publications.   (120)

ELKINS, W.F. "The Influence of Marcus Garvey on Africa: A
British Report of 1922." In: Science and Society, New York,
Summer 1968, pp. 321-323.   (121)

EMERSON, RUPERT. Africa and U.S. Foreign Policy. Englewood
Cliffs, N.J., Prentice-Hall, 1967, 117 pp.   (122)

_____. "Race in Africa: United States Foreign Policy." In:
George Shepherd (ed.), Racial Influences on American Foreign
Policy. New York, Basic Books, 1970, pp. 165-185. Inter-
esting general discussion of American policies toward Africa

and how they are perceived by Afro-Americans. Says that
although Blacks here are still not, on the whole, very
knowledgeable about Africa, such awareness is increasing as
Blacks realize that both here and in Africa it is a case of
haves vs. have-nots. On the other hand, Emerson concedes
that Black Americans are not sufficiently concerned about
Africa so that they can be relied upon as a voting bloc on
matters pertaining to that continent. Says that the roots
of identity have been obscured by the passage of time and
that an increase in such identification will take place
only if there is no improvement in the lives of Black people
in the United States. Points out that Swahili is an East
African language but is used in the United States largely
as a symbolic form of identifying with Africa and that in
general, identity with Africa is symbolic. (123)

EMERSON, RUPERT AND MATRIN KILSON. "The Rise of Africa and
the Negro American." In: Daedalus, Fall 1965, pp. 1055-
1084. Discussion of the effects that the emergence of independent African states have had upon Afro-Americans. Among
influences are pride, psychological well-being, and sense of
importance. A bit dated by now. (124)

ENGO, PAUL B. "On African Liberation and the Role of the
Black Woman in America." In: Pan African Journal, Nairobi,
Vol. 4, No. 2, 1971, pp. 151-157. (125)

EPPS, ARCHIE. "A Negro Separatist Movement of the 19th
Century." In: Harvard Review, Cambridge, Mass., Summer 1969,
pp. 69-87. Discussion of the separatist activities engaged
in by the African Methodist Episcopal Church during the 19th
Century. Intended to refute the popularly held notion that
the church cared little about its' members' needs. (126)

_____. "The Theme of Exile in Malcolm X's Harvard Speeches."
In: Harvard Journal of Negro Affairs, Cambridge, Mass.,
Vol. 2, No. 1, 1968, pp. 40-54. Critical analysis of three
speeches given by Malcolm X at Harvard University. Points
out that in advocating the idea of a Black homeland Malcolm
X had in mind, in the following order, three places: the
Moslem world, some place in the United States, and lastly,
Africa. Publicly Malcolm X called for revolution but pri-
vately he desired escape, speculates Epps. According to
the author's interpretation, Malcolm X's ideas on Afro-Americans and Africa were romantic, a result of his long involvement with the Black Muslims and, after that, Black nationalism. Because of this, argues Epps, he was a poor choice to
deal with political problems that, above all, required great
realism. (127)

ESSIEN-UDOM, E.U. "Black Identity in the International Context."
In: Nathan I. Huggins, Martin Kilson, and Daniel M. Fox (eds.),
Key Issues in the Afro-American Experience. (Vol. II), New
York, Harcourt, Brace, Johanovich, 1971, pp. 223-258. Good
summary of the historical interest and involvement of Afro-

Americans with Africa.   (128)

_____. "Introduction." In: Amy Jacques Garvey, Philosophy and Opinions of Marcus Garvey. London, Frank Cass Ltd.,   (129)

_____. "The Nationalist Movements of Harlem." In: Freedomways, New York, Summer 1963, pp. 335-342. Although primarily a descriptive article, author makes a number of important points as well. In an essentially pessimistic appraisal of the present and future status of Black nationalist groups, author observes that, with the exception of the Black Muslims, none of the organizations are really very effectively run and that they have many differences among themselves. Writer notes that the past track record of such groups is a poor one. At the same time, Essien-Udom believes that an appreciation of the past is essential for the true freedom of Black Americans. Author also reminds us that whereas the Muslims are basically a religious movement, most Black nationalist groups have been political in orientation i.e. land, political party, etc.. (130)

ESSIEN-UDOM, RUBY M. AND E.U. ESSIEN-UDOM. In: John H. Clarke (ed.), Malcolm X: The Man and his Times. New York, Colliers, 1969, pp. 235-267. Drawing heavily on his speeches, writings, and experiences, the authors attempt to demonstrate that Malcolm X was basically a Pan-Africanist who viewed the Third World struggle as an integral part of the Afro-American struggle. Although he was a revolutionary socialist who saw the need for unity among the black, red, yellow, and brown races of the world, he was especially concerned with the future of Africa and the need for a dialogue between Afro-Americans and Africans. Authors date this attitude from his break with Elijah Muhammad, stating that earlier in his life he had not yet developed an international perspective. As an example of this view, they talk about Malcolm X's attempts to convince African leaders to bring charges against the United States for violations of human rights. Finally, they also discuss his group, the Organization of Afro-American Unity and his involvement with the Organization of African Unity.   (131)

FARAH, ABULRAHIM A.. "A Remembrance on African Liberation Day of Our Heritage." In: Pan-African Journal, Nairobi, Vol. 4, No. 2, 1971, pp. 168-172.   (132)

FARMER, JAMES. "An American Negro Leader's View of African Unity." In: African Forum, New York, Summer 1965, pp. 69-89. Farmer reports on a trip made in February 1965 to eight African countries in which he found the African attitude towards the United States somewhat distrustful largely because of American policies toward the Congo, South Africa, and elsewhere, and also because of its policies toward Blacks in the United States. Says that the origins of both the Civil Rights Movement and the African independence movements are to be found in World War II when much of Europe and the United States was involved in the fight against the

Nazis and their racial theories. Farmer asserts that both
leaders and masses in Africa "were unanimous in viewing
American Negroes as their brothers" (p. 74) and that reports
of mutual feelings of contempt were completely false. While
reports of hostility are no doubt exaggerated, it is felt
that the converse, as suggested by Farmer, paints an overly
rosy picture. Perhaps it was his sponsorship by AMSAC, an
organization that is heavily involved in Afro-American –
African activities or possibly it was because of the people
he was exposed to. Whatever, there are Afro-Americans and
Africans who look at each other with something less than
brotherly love and there are some problems between the two
groups. Farmer should at least have mentioned the other
side of the picture. Farmer also calls for cultural exchange
programs with Africa, pressure by organized groups of Blacks
on the United States to influence African policy by this
government, more visits to Africa by Blacks, and more diplo-
matic appointments of Afro-Americans to African lands.   (133)

FAX, ELTON. Garvey: The Story of a Pioneer Black Nationalist.
Fax's biography of Garvey treats his life in the context of
West Indian and Jamaican history. Writing in an interesting
style, Fax draws upon earlier works such as Amy Jacques
Garvey, and Edmund David Cronon in interpreting various events
in Garvey's life. A good book.   (134)

FEELINGS, TOM. "A Letter from Tom Feelings to Julian Mayfield."
In: Black World, Chicago, Ill., August 1971, pp. 26-34.   (135)

FIERCE, MILFRED C. "Africa --- Some Views and Previews." In:
Negro History Bulletin, Washington, D.C., April 1972, pp. 78-
79.   (136)

FINNEY, RON. "'We are All Babylonians': Afro-Americans in
Africa." In: Black Scholar, San Francisco, Calif., February
1973, pp. 45-48. Brief, yet highly illuminating account of
an Afro-American's experiences in Africa while there on a
visit. Author, a graduate student at the University of
California at Los Angeles and former editor of Black Voice,
talks about the middle-class composition of most Afro-Americans who visit Africa and notes how unrepresentative they
are of most Blacks in the United States. Asserts that many,
if not the majority of Africans see little or no difference
between Black Americans and white Americans. We might add
parenthetically that Africans who come to the United States
are not representative either of most of their countrymen
and that it might be very interesting if more ways could be
found to increase the contact between the less-advantaged
members of both groups.   (137)

FISHEL, LESLIE H. JR. AND BENJAMIN QUARLES. The Negro American: A Documentary History. Glenview, Ill., Scott, Foresman,
and Co., 1967, 536 pp.   (138)

FONLON, BERNARD. "The Passing of a Great African." In:

<u>Freedomways</u>, New York, Winter 1965, pp. 195-206. Written
by a native of Cameroon, article eulogizes W.E.B. Du Bois,
praising him for his role in the development of Pan-Africanism and for his early support of it.   (139)

FORMAN, JAMES. "The Concept of International Black Power."
In: <u>Pan-African Journal</u>, Nairobi, Spring & Summer 1968,
pp. 92-95. Black power is international, argues Forman,
since it encompasses Blacks everywhere and Black people in
the United States should be called Africans, not Afro-Americans since they are not American citizens. Article includes
a number of concrete proposals for enhancing African-Afro-
American relations: 1. More Blacks should visit Africa
and learn about its culture. 2. Ideas from both continents
should be exchanged and published. 3. Afro-Americans should
give to Africa by lending it their technical skills. Forman
says that hostility and suspicion between Afro-Americans and
Africans has been fostered by the United States and by re-
actionary African countries such as Malawi who would like to
keep the two groups separate. Does not expand on this last
statement.   (140)

_____. "Black Manifesto." In: <u>Pan-African Journal</u>, Fall
1969, pp. 421-431. The Manifesto was delivered at the
National Black Economic Development Conference held in
April 1969 in Detroit, Michigan. While perhaps best known
for its demands for reparations, the Manifesto also contains
some interesting points with respect to Africa. Forman criticizes Blacks for not taking enough interest in Africa, for
not being willing to give of their skills to Africa, and
says that by **virtue** of living in the United States they have
an opportunity to help destroy a major source of world
exploitation.   (141)

FOSTER, BADI G. "United States Foreign Policy Toward Africa:
An Afro-American Perspective." In: <u>Issue</u>, Waltham, Mass.,
Summer 1972, pp. 45-51. Good article that argues that
Blacks have always been interested in Africa and that the
concern shown today is merely a continuation of past interest. Foster says that Black Americans are suspicious of
United States policy in Africa, especially its failure to
take stronger action against South Africa. Sees the situation in South Africa as a potential unifying force between
the Black intellectual elite (whom, he asserts, are the ones
now taking the most interest in Africa) and the masses.
Urges the United States government to put more Blacks in
policy-making positions and to show greater interest in
Africa.   (142)

FOX, RICHARD W. "Black Panthers in Africa." In: <u>Common-
weal</u>, October 3, 1969, pp. 6-7.   (143)

FRIEDMAN, NEIL. "Africa and the Afro-American: The Changing
Negro Identity." In: <u>Psychiatry</u>, Washington, D.C., May
1969, pp. 127-136. Attempts to tie in the past negative self-

identification that existed among many Blacks to their negative images of Africa. Relying heavily on quotes from
Harold R. Isaacs' book, The New World of Negro Americans,
to substantiate the existence of this image, Friedman states
that this has deprived the Black American of a crucial alternative form of positive identification which he might have
used as a defense mechanism against the negative self-image
projected on him by whites. Author cites Isaacs in pointing
the blame for negative images of Africa at missionaries,
schools, and the media. Friedman notes that the emergence
of Africa has resulted in Blacks viewing themselves more
positively, i.e. Afros, pride in skin color, etc.. Black
identity as a whole is therefore undergoing important
changes.   (144)

"Full Circle --- Black Americans Relate to Africa." In:
Negro History Bulletin, Washington, D.C., April 1972,
pp. 76-78 (editorial).   (145)

FULLER, HOYT W. Journey to Africa. Chicago, Ill., Third
World Press, 1971, 95 pp. Personal account of a Black
American's experiences while living in Africa for eleven
years, mostly in Guinea and Senegal. Talks about the importance of establishing ties between Afro-Americans and Africans. Is sharply critical of the Black bourgeoisie from the
United States who, he charges, are, in many cases, exploiting
Africans. Also levels the familiar charge that AMSAC was
CIA-supported. While not especially analytical, this is a
good descriptive account of life in Africa as seen through
the eyes of a Black American.   (146)

FYFE, CHRISTOPHER. A History of Sierra Leone. London,
Oxford University Press, 1962, 773 pp. Although the involvement of Afro-Americans in the development of Sierra
Leone was not as great as in Liberia, there were quite a
few Blacks who emigrated to that country. Among them was
a group of 1190 ex-slaves who had been freed by the British,
had resettled in Nova Scotia, and had eventually emigrated
to Sierra Leone. Others came from the United States via
England. These and other migrations to Sierra Leone are
detailed in this authoritative history of Sierra Leone.   (147)

GARLAND, PHYL. "Soul to Soul." In: Ebony, Chicago, Ill.,
June 1971, p. 79.   (148)

_____. "Is the Afro On the Way Out?" In: Ebony, Chicago,
Ill., February 1973, pp. 128-136.   (149)

GARRETT, ROMEO B. "African Survivals in American Culture."
In: Journal of Negro History, Washington, D.C., October
1966, pp. 239-245. Rather short yet interesting discussion
of the African origins of American songs, dances, words,
instruments, stories, and foods. Words like tote, tater,
chimpanzee, the word "juke" as in jukebox, have African
origins. The rhumba, mambo, conga, and Charleston were

originally African. Different tales such as Uncle Remus and
other animal tales are of African extraction. Black-eyed
peas were the food eaten by Black slaves during the middle
passage from Africa. Watermelon is still found growing wild
in Africa. Coffee comes from Kaffa, Ethiopia,and Kola was
originally an African drink. Garrett does not talk about
Afro-American wood objects, pottery, etc.. Still this is
an excellent source for lecture material on the African heritage in the Black experience.   (150)

GARVEY, AMY JACQUES. Black Power in America. Kingston,
Jamaica, 1968, 42 pp.   (151)

_____. Garvey and Garveyism. Kingston, Jamaica, 1963,
287 pp. Biography of Marcus M. Garvey that contains, among
other things, a fairly detailed discussion of his abortive
attempts at colonization in Liberia (pp. 140-149). While
some may question Garvey's actual intentions insofar as
settling in Liberia was concerned, a reading of this work
leaves little doubt that Garvey played a central role in
giving publicity to Africa and in making Black people proud
of it. Book also brings together many quotes from Garvey
that show his emphasis on the importance of Africa.   (152)

_____. "Garvey and Garveyism: A Wife's Footnote to Black
History." In: Black World, Chicago, Ill., February 1971,
pp. 75-76.   (153)

_____. Garvey and Pan-Africanism: A Wife's Footnote to
Black History." In: Black World, Chicago, Ill., December
1971, pp. 15-18.   (154)

_____. "Marcus Mosiah Garvey." In: Negro Digest, Chicago,
Ill., May 1969, p. 42.   (155)

_____. The Philosophy and Opinions of Marcus Garvey. 2nd ed.,
London, Frank Cass, 1967, 2 vols. Invaluable source for
those interested in Garvey. Basically a collection of his
speeches, writings, and extracts from his trial. It was
edited by his wife with the first volume appearing in 1923
and the second in 1925. This particular edition contains
a very good introduction by E.U. Essien-Udom about Garvey's
life. In one of his speeches Garvey argued that African
freedom depended in good part on the technological and
scientific contributions of Blacks in America (p. 43).
Talked about the need to build an empire in Africa and was
sharply critical of those who said it was insect-ridden and
too hot (p. 50). Discussed emigration to Africa and caution-
ed Afro-Americans to treat Africans equally (p. 52). Throughout the entire work Garvey criticizes and condemns white
colonization. Garvey also states, in urging Blacks to return
to Africa that "the thoughtful and industrious of our race
want to go back to Africa because we realize it will be our
only hope of permanent existence." (p. 122, vol. 2). There
is also a valuable and detailed account of Garvey's efforts

to secure agreements with Liberia and the problems he
encountered buying land. He accuses the Liberian government of having sold out to the Firestone Rubber Company and
to European interests.   (156)

GENOVESE, EUGENE D. "The Negro Laborer in Africa and in the
Slave South." In: <u>Phylon,</u> Atlanta, Ga., Winter 1960,
pp. 343-350. Deals with the assertion by Ulrich B. Phillips
and others that African culture was inferior and that Blacks
needed to be taught discipline in order to become good
workers on the plantation. Genovese's arguments include:
If Black was not fit for agricultural work, then why was he
brought here at all? Moreover, Africans had slavery and the
Black worker here was therefore already domesticated. Finally,
Genovese points out that Ashanti, Yoruba, and other tribes
had highly developed agricultural systems.   (157)

GIBSON, RICHARD LEE. "South African Toms Denounce Stokely."
In: <u>Liberator,</u> December 1967, pp. 10-11.   (158)

GILES, RAYMOND H. JR. <u>Black and Ethnic Studies Programs at</u>
<u>Public Schools: Elementary and Secondary.</u> Amherst, Mass.,
Center for International Education, School of Education,
1972, 188 pp., especially pp. 29-57. Examination of a number
of ethnic and Black studies programs. Most interesting for
our topic is the section called "Images of Africa." Giles
conducted a study in Spring 1969 which found that Black
Harlem schoolchildren (grades 4, 5, and 6) were not positively oriented towards Africa even after an intensive, nine-
month African heritage program. The various classes sampled
were taught by three different types of people --- an African
male, an Afro-American female, and a white male. Giles questions whether pride can be taught in the school system as
it is presently constituted. He also suggests that the children's negative attitudes are shaped by white culture long before he or she begins attending school. Author argues that
such programs should concentrate as much on the very real
differences in culture as on the similarities between Afro-
Americans and Africans. Teachers should make efforts to
dispel commonly-held myths and stereotypes about Africa.
Essentially a good study although it does have one important
weakness: Giles fails to describe the course content in any
depth. Also, future research in this area might focus on
the attitudes of pre-school children to pin-point the effects
of white racism and how such programs alter the child's perception. Even here, Giles should have interviewed the children <u>before</u> they began the program.   (159)

GOINS, ALVIN E. AND MAX MEENES. "Ethnic and Class Preferences
Among College Negroes." In: <u>Journal of Negro Education,</u>
Washington, D.C., Spring 1960, pp. 128-133.   (160)

GOLDMAN, PETER. <u>The Death and Life of Malcolm X.</u> New York,
Harper & Row, 1973, 438 pp. Solid book containing an excellent section on Malcolm X's two trips to Africa. Goldman

asserts that Malcolm X was a Black nationalist first and then a socialist and that he was impressed by African socialism. Author presents a sensitive portrayal of the doubts and ambivalent feelings that marked this great man's life particularly around the time he was leaving the Black Muslims. There are interesting accounts of Malcolm X's visit to Cairo, his rather disappointing meeting with Kwame Nkrumah in 1964, and his surprise at not finding only Blacks working in top positions in Africa. (161)

GOODMAN, GEORGE. "Harlem's Yorubas." In: Look, January 7, 1969, pp. 32-33. (162)

GOODWIN, EVERETT E. "Africa and Afro-American Identity: Problems and Prospects." In: Black World, Chicago, Ill., May 1973, p. 37. (163)

GORDON, JACOB U. "Black America and Recent African Civilization." In: Afro-American Studies, New York, Vol. 1, No. 3, 1971, pp. 221-225. (164)

HALEY, ALEX. "My Furthest Back Person --- 'The African.'" In: New York Times, New York, July 16, 1972, Section Six, pp. 13-16. Excellent example of how the 1960s affected Black people. Although he had been hearing about his African great-great-great-great grandfather ever since he was a small child, Haley had never done anything with that knowledge. Finally, in 1965, Haley began his search for his ancestors, a search that ended successfully in West Africa. While it is true that many Afro-Americans would be unable to duplicate Haley's feat, his experience shows that it can be done, in addition to graphically illustrating the Afro-American's past and heritage. (165)

HALL, GWENDOLYN M. "Africans in the Americas." In: Negro Digest, Chicago, Ill., February 1969, pp. 35-44. (166)

HAMILTON, CHARLES V. "Pan-Africanism and the Black Struggle in the U.S.." In: Black Scholar, San Francisco, Calif., March 1971, pp. 10-15. Good article on how the Afro-American and African struggles are interrelated. Says that although the most important areas for Blacks in this country are jobs, housing, education, and political power, these are not merely reformist goals but part of the world-wide, Pan-African struggle. This is so, says Hamilton, because if Black Americans are to have any real influence on American policies in Africa, they must first acquire political and economic clout at home. (167)

HANSBERRY, WILLIAM L. "W.E.B. Du Bois' Influence on African History." In: Freedomways, New York, Winter 1965, pp. 73-87. Well-written and informative discussion of Du Bois' scholarly contributions to an understanding of Africa's past. Writer also mentions how he and others were influenced by Du Bois in terms of their own interest in this topic. (168)

HARE, NATHAN. "Wherever We Are." In: Black Scholar, San
Francisco, Calif., March 1971, pp. 34-37.   (169)

HARGREAVES, JOHN D. "African Colonization in the Nineteenth
Century --- Liberia and Sierra Leone." In: Jeffrey Butler
(ed.), Boston University Papers in African History, Vol. 1,
Boston, Mass., Boston University Press, 1964, pp. 55-76.   (170)

HARLAN, LOUIS R. "Booker T. Washington and the White Man's
Burden." In: American Historical Review, Washington, D.C.,
January 1966, pp. 441-467. Thoughts about Black leaders of
the past who emphasized Africa in the Twentieth Century
often lead to Marcus Garvey and W.E.B. Du Bois, among others.
Therefore, this fine article detailing Booker T. Washington's
interest in and involvement with Africa is most welcome and
worthwhile. Talks about Tuskegeeans going as farmers to
Togo in the beginning of the Twentieth Century, Washington's
attempts to use his influence with President Roosevelt to
improve conditions for Blacks in the Congo, and his efforts
to prevent Liberia from being swallowed up by European colonialists (England, Germany, and France). Harlan concludes,
however, that Washington's conservatism extended to his
attitudes toward Africa and that, in principle at least, he
supported colonialism there. This was true, according to
Harlan, of Liberia too where he encouraged American investment in that land.   (171)

HARRIS, JOSEPH E. "Introduction to the African Diaspora."
In: T.O. Ranger (ed.), Emerging Themes of African History,
London, Heinemann Educational Books Ltd., 1966, pp. 147-
151.   (172)

HARRIS, SHELDON H. "An American's Impressions of Sierra Leone
in 1811." In: Journal of Negro History, Washington, D.C.,
January 1962, pp. 35-41.   (173)

_____. Paul Cuffe: Black America and the African Return.
New York, Simon and Schuster, 1972. 288 pp. Biography of
Paul Cuffe, a wealthy Black merchant who is generally con-
sidered one of the first Black emigrationists to Africa
(Sierra Leone). Two-thirds of the book consists of Cuffe's
diary and his letters. Those interested in learning about
Cuffe and the sort of man he was should definitely read
this well-written and thorough account.   (174)

HART, RICHARD. "The Life and Resurrection of Marcus Garvey."
In: Race, London, Vol. 9, No. 2, 1967, pp. 217-237.   (175)

HATCH, JOHN. "Americans -- Or Exiled Africans?" In:
Listener, London, September 9, 1965, pp. 365-367.   (176)

HENRIKSEN, THOMAS H. "Edward W. Blyden: His Influence on
Contemporary Afro-Americans." In: Pan-African Journal,
Nairobi, Summer 1971, pp. 255-265. Looks at Blyden's
writings and tries to show how they influenced Afro-Ameri-

37

cans today and how the ideas reached the United States.
Blyden felt that Africans had a highly developed sense
of spirituality. Henriksen points out (as does Hollis
Lynch) that Blyden's efforts in developing Pan-Negroism
were the basis for what later became Pan-Africanism.
Article also evaluates the influence of Blyden's ideas
on Garvey, Du Bois, Malcolm X, and others.   (177)

HERSKOVITZ, MELVILLE J. A Historical Approach to Afro-
American Studies: A Critique." In: American Anthropologist, Washington, D.C., August 1960, pp. 559-568.
Attack on those who would require pure retention of Africanisms before agreeing that a New World culture was African in origin. Argues for greater emphasis on such retentions in the study of Afro-American culture and that of
Black people living in other parts of the New World.   (178)

_____. The Myth of the Negro Past. Boston, Mass., Beacon
Press, 1958, 368 pp. This classic, originally published
in 1941 and reprinted in 1958, is required reading for anyone who undertakes to understand the Afro-American's relationship to Africa, hence its inclusion in this bibliography
despite its pre-1960 publication date. This edition also
contains a new introduction by the author. Generally
speaking, the book is a provocative and far-ranging discussion of African survivals among Blacks in the New World.
While many of Herskovitz's assertions concerning secular
retentions of Africanisms are somewhat speculative and open
to question, on the whole, this book is quite successful in
refuting the then popularly-held notion that Black people
lost their culture or had none when they arrived on these
shores.   (179)

HERO, ALFRED O. JR. "American Negroes and U.S. Foreign Policy:
1937-1967." In: Journal of Conflict Resolution, Beverly
Hills, Calif., Vol. 13, No. 2, 1969, pp. 220-251.   (180)

HICKS, E. PERRY AND BARRY K. BEYER. "Images of Africa." In:
Journal of Negro Education, Washington, D.C., Spring 1970,
pp. 158-166. Report of a study of attitudes toward Africa
south of the Sahara by secondary school students (seventh and
and twelfth graders). Study concludes that while students
do know something about Africa, they also have many misconceptions ranging from the belief that Timbuctu is famous for
its diamonds (rather than universities) to "most of Africa
south of the Sahara is covered by jungles rather than grass-
lands." This despite the fact that most students have presumably learned something about Africa by the time they
reach the twelfth grade. Interestingly, a higher percentage
of twelfth graders had misconceptions than seventh graders.
Study criticizes school programs for their superficiality
and cites the need for improving their content. This is
based on a 1967 sample and we have every reason to expect
that programs today are far better. It would have been
good had the authors given a racial breakdown of the group

sampled. Nonetheless, this article is quite useful for
educators in the field.   (181)

HICKS, JOHN H. "Negroes and African Nationalism." In:
Social Order, April 1961, pp. 150-155.   (182)

HILL, ADELAIDE C. "The Dilemma of the Afro-American." In:
Afro-American Studies, New York, December 1971, pp. 187-
189. Interesting article which argues that while Black
Americans are racially and historically of African origin,
their culture is basically American since they have been
here for quite some time. Although both groups do have in
common the history of aggression in the form of colonization,
Hill takes the position that Afro-Americans should come to
grips with this reality by enhancing and developing a culture and lifestyle that is reflective of their total (both
African and American) experience rather than becoming completely separatist. It would have been considerably more
helpful had Hill specified what aspects of Afro-American
culture emanate from the different experiences and made some
concrete suggestions on how they could be fused to form a
successful amalgamation of the two.   (183)

_____. "What is Africa to Us?" In: Floyd Barbour (ed.),
The Black Power Revolt. Boston, Mass., Porter-Sargent,
1968, pp. 127-135.   (184)

HOADLEY, J. STEPHEN. "Black Americans and U.S. Policy Toward
Africa." In: Journal of Black Studies, Beverly Hills,
Calif., June 1972, pp. 489-502. Interesting study of
attitudes toward Africa conducted in St. Louis, Missouri
Based on a questionnaire, writer concludes that among Blacks
and whites who are interested in Africa, Blacks have more
positive attitudes toward the continent and that young
Blacks favor a more active role in shaping policy toward
Africa (as opposed to older members of the Black community).
Whites were somewhat reluctant to have Afro-Americans only
consulted about African matters. Hoadley concludes that
the general lack of enthusiasm for Africa expressed by whites
may indicate that it will be harder for Black Americans to
shape policy toward Africa in the future. Study also included a content analysis of articles that appeared in Black
and white newspapers concerning Africa. Hoadley found more
articles on Africa in white papers than in Black publications
and concluded therefore that Blacks, in general, are not more
interested in Africa than whites. While it is possible that
this is true, the statement is not justified from the evidence
presented. Black newspapers represent primarily the interests
of the Black middle-class and are not indicative of the views
of younger elements who, Hoadley himself indicates, are more
interested in Africa. In any event, a similar study today
might well conclude that even the Black middle-class is more
concerned with the African continent.   (185)

HOFFER, ERIC. "The Negro is Against Himself." In: New York

<u>Times</u>, New York, November 29, 1964, Section Six, p. 27.   (186)

HOLDEN, EDITH. <u>Blyden of Liberia: An Account of the Life and
Labor of Edward Wilmot Blyden, L.L.D., as Recorded in Letters
and in Print</u>. New York, Vantage Press, 1966, 1040 pp.
Lengthy account of Blyden's life relying quite heavily on
Blyden's letters and other, printed sources. Descriptive,
not analytical.   (187)

HOLLOWAY, MARVIN. "The Search for Identity: Social and Poli-
tical Protest Movements." In: Inez Smith Reid (ed.), <u>The
Black Prism: Perspectives on the Black Experience</u>, New
York, Faculty Press, 1969, pp. 97-101.   (188)

HOOKER, J.R. "The Negro American Press and Africa in the
Nineteen Thirties." In: <u>Canadian Journal of African Studies</u>,
Ottawa, March 1967, pp. 43-50. **Discussion** of how Africa was
perceived by the Black press in the 1930s. Author divides
these perceptions into the following four areas: 1. Africa
as an embarrassment -- stereotyped picture of Africa -- canni-
bals, naked savages, etc. and a good deal of attention given
to the efforts of missionaries there. 2. Africa as a zone
of exploitation -- many articles portrayed Africa as a place
where a person could make a quick financial killing. 3. As
the symbol of white injustice - focused largely on the Italian-Ethiopian War. 4. As redemption - not the missionary
style of the Nineteenth Century but rather a stressing of the
African heritage, culture, and history. One of only a few
articles on this subject. Marred a bit by superficiality.
Hooker presents only brief and scattered references to support
his evaluation, as opposed to a more systematic examination.
                                                            (189)

House of Representatives. <u>Policy Toward Africa for the Seven-
ties. Hearings Before the Subcommittee on Africa of the
Committee on Foreign Affairs</u>. Ninety-First Congress, Second
Session, Washington, D.C., pp. 54-93; 251-293.   (190)

HOWARD, CHARLES P. SR. "How the Press Defames Africa." In:
<u>Freedomways</u>, New York, Fall 1962, pp. 361-370. Citing the
poor publicity given Patrice Lumumba, former leader in the
Congo, Howard attacks the treatment accorded Africa by the
American and European press. Says African countries are
condemned or praised according to cold war interests.   (191)

HOWE, RUSSELL W. "A Reply to Horace Mann Bond." In: <u>Negro
History Bulletin</u>, Washington, D.C., February 1962, pp. 102-
104. In a response to Bond's criticism of his original
article (See HORACE M. BOND, "Howe and Isaacs in the Bush:
The Ram in the Thicket."), Howe insists that Afro-Americans
have no more in common with Africans than whites except,
perhaps, in a historical sense. Those who do, says Howe,
are the exceptions to the rule: "Leopold Senghor is more
like General De Gaulle than Horace Mann Bond."   (192)

_____. "Strangers in Africa." In: <u>Reporter</u>, London, June 22, 1961, pp. 34-35. Criticizes use of Black Americans as professionals in Africa. Argues that Africans see the Afro-American as a descendant of slaves, who, while he is Black, is unable to speak the tribal language. Africans are also critical of Afro-Americans for having failed to obtain full rights from the white man after all these years. Moreover, they sense that Black Americans are uneasy in this culture. Howe admits that some Blacks have acclimated well in Africa. Aside from the basic issue of whether or not these views are really shared by the majority of Africans (even in 1961 and certainly in 1976) Howe ignores the fact that these are stereotypes resulting from ignorance which could probably be most easily worked out through increased contact and through cultural exchange programs. See also HORACE M. BOND "Howe and Isaacs in the Bush: The Ram in the Thicket." (193)

HUGGINS, NATHAN I. <u>Harlem Renaissance</u>. New York, Oxford University Press, 1971, 343 pp. As part of a larger discussion of the Harlem scene in the 1920s, Huggins talks about the efforts of the Renaissance to forge cultural links between Africa and the Afro-American experience. While Huggins does discuss the roles played by Du Bois and Garvey in connection with Africa, his account is most valuable for its portrayal of the interest in Africa evinced by Renaissance intellectuals such as Alain Locke, Aaron Douglas, Countee Cullen, Langston Hughes, etc.. (194)

_____. "Pilgrimage for Black Americans: The Slave Castles of West Africa." In: <u>New York Times</u>, New York, Section Ten, October 29, 1972, pp. 1, 13. Written in a popular style that is clearly intended for mass consumption, this interesting little piece talks about the slave castles, particularly Elmina, and what it feels like, as an Afro-American to go there. Especially useful if you plan on making the trip. (195)

ISAACS, HAROLD R. "Back to Africa." In: <u>New Yorker</u>, New York, May 13, 1961, pp. 105-143. Interesting, lengthy, yet somewhat impressionistic discourse on the problems facing Afro-Americans living in Africa. Isaacs states that as alien as Blacks may feel in America there are many aspects of life in Africa that will make them uncomfortable there too, i.e. attitudes toward servants and the role of women in marriage. Author quotes Black Americans who feel they should receive "special attention." Cites others who believe they are looked down upon because they do not possess a French or British education, try to be white, and have not been sufficiently aggressive in the Civil Rights Movement. Aside from the article's datedness, Isaacs appears to misperceive lack of commitment to Africa by certain Afro-Americans as a sign of basic incompatibility. See HORACE M. BOND annotation. (196)

_____. "Blackness and Whiteness." In: <u>Encounter</u>, Indianapolis, Ind., August 1963, pp. 8-21.   (197)

_____. "Du Bois and Africa." In: <u>Race</u>, London, November
1960, pp. 3-23. Good article based on interview conducted
by Isaacs with Du Bois when the latter was ninety-two years
old. Discusses Du Bois' writings on the subject and his
first visit to Africa in 1923. Argues that although Du
Bois was a "romantic racist", he never urged mass migration
to Africa. Rather he tried to promote the freedom of Africa for Africans.   (198)

_____. <u>Emergent Americans: A Report on Crossroads Africa</u>.
New York, John Day, 1962, 158 pp. Report on the experiences
of a group of young Americans, among whom were quite a few
Blacks, while spending a summer working in various African
communities.   (199)

_____. "Five Writers and their African Ancestors." In:
<u>Phylon</u>, Atlanta, Ga., Fall 1960, pp. 243-265.   (200)

_____. "Five Writers and their African Ancestors: Part II."
In: <u>Phylon</u>, Atlanta, Ga., Winter 1960, pp. 317-336.   (201)

_____. <u>The New World of Negro Americans</u>. New York, John Day,
1963, 366 pp. In this well-known book, the author concludes,
on the basis of 107 in-depth interviews with prominent Afro-
Americans, that Black people have generally been ashamed of
Africa and are either not interested in, or disillusioned
about it. Furthermore, Isaacs asserts that there is no real
basis for the establishment of closer ties between the two
groups. Although highly provocative and interesting, the
book's value is diminished by several methodological limita-
tions. To begin with, the interviews were not systematically
carried out. In addition, the selection of elite members of
the community makes the book unrepresentative of the general
Black population in this country. Finally, the interviews
are nowhere given in their complete form, not even in an
appendix. As a result, there is no way of knowing in what
context the statements quoted by Isaacs were made.   (202)

JACKSON, LARRY R. "The Mutual Reciprocity between the African
and Afro-American Revolutions." In: <u>Afro-American Studies</u>,
New York, Vol. 2, No. 1, 1971, pp. 1-13.   (203)

JAHN, JAHNHEINZ. <u>Muntu: The New African Culture</u>. New York,
Grove Press, 1961, 267 pp. Classic work dealing with African culture. Jahn makes a number of interesting observations
relevant to the Afro-American experience as part of a larger
discussion of African culture around the world. In his
chapter on blues, he says that there is a tendency for literature and music to move away from African styles, largely because of the passage of time. Jahn points out a number of
important distinctions concerning these survivals. He con-
trasts the Christian idea of man's obedience to God with the
African one of man creating his God through "active worship"

(p. 219). Yet, Jahn notes, in terms of music, rhythm, etc.,
there are many similarities (the difference is in attitude;
the Christian view is subservient, the African dominant).
Jahn observes that in African music the singing accompanies
the drums whereas in Afro-American blues the opposite prevails. The singer leads and the instruments accompany (p.
221). In a pessimistic appraisal, Jahn defines the Black
situation here as culturally hopeless because he only wants
to be a full American and is, in reality, differentiated by
skin color alone. Author also asserts that Black American
novels, i.e. Invisible Man, Go Tell it on the Mountain, and
Native Son are not at all similar to African novels because
they focus primarily on the dilemmas of split personalities
and inferiority complexes, problems essentially Afro-American (in a racial sense, at least). It is hardly necessary
to point out that times have changed since 1961, and with
them Black pride, identity, and the form of the Black novel
Still, it is surprising that so a perceptive a researcher
as Jahn should have considered the position of Afro-Americans so bleak in 1958 (the book was only translated in 1961).
In addition to its careful and penetrating picture of African culture, this work provides one with an opportunity to
retrospectively appreciate the achievements of Afro-Americans
since the early 1960s.   (204)

_____. Neo-African Literature. New York, Grove Press, 1968,
301 pp., especially pp. 182-191.   (205)

JAMES C.L.R. A History of Pan-African Revolt. Washington,
D.C., Drum and Spear Press, (Second edition, revised), 1969,
151 pp.   (206)

"James Forman of S.N.C.C. Addresses the United Nations."
In: Liberator, December 1967, pp. 8-9.   (207)

JEANPIERRE, W.A. "African Negritude --- Black American Soul."
In: Africa Today, Denver, Col., December 1967, pp. 10-11.
Comparative evaluation of Negritude and Soul. Negritude,
as expressed by Senghor and Cesaire, is seen as an intellectual movement, and Soul, which developed more recently, is
viewed as its counterpart for the Afro-American masses.
Both are positive affirmations in response to experiences
with whites; both deal directly with the essence of Blackness. Article does not discuss how Negritude directly or
indirectly influenced Soul.   (208)

JOANS, TED. "First Papers on Ancestral Creations." In:
Black World, Chicago, Ill., August 1970, pp. 66-72.   (209)

_____. "Natural Africa." In: Black World, Chicago, Ill.,
May 1971, pp. 4-7.   (210)

JOHNSON, W.R. "Afro-American and Southern Africa." In:
Africa Today, Denver, Col., Summer 1972. Traces the historical relationship between Afro-Americans and South Afri-

cans, particularly through the A.M.E. Church noting that
the two groups have been in contact for almost 100 years.
Urges present-day support for the South African liberation
struggle because he sees the position of Black Americans
as being enhanced by the existence of a strong and independent Black Africa. Says that the plight of South Africa's Black population should be effectively publicized,
that Afro-Americans should provide technical assistance
and financial aid, rather than simply giving lip service
to the Black struggle for freedom in that country.   (211)

_____. "Do Negroes and Africans Really Dig Each Other?"
In: Negro Digest, Chicago, Ill., May 1962, pp. 83-87.   (212)

JONES, HANNA A.B. The Struggle for Political and Cultural
Unification in Liberia, 1847-1930. Evanston, Ill., Northwestern University, 1962, 315 1.   (213)

See also Nos. 23-27.
JONES, LE ROI (IMAMU AMIRI BARAKA). Blues People. New York,
William Morrow and Company, 1963, 244 pp. Evaluates the
development of Afro-American music through history. Includes an excellent discussion of Africanisms with some
very perceptive observations: Religion, music, and dance
forms were more likely to survive than iron-working, wood
carving, and the like because they were not as material in
form. Jones gives specific examples of how African culture
survived in the United States among Black people i.e. Rhythm
came from the use of drums to communicate by phonetically
reproducing the words. This required great rhythmic sensitivity. Says that Afro-Americans adopted Christianity
because their own religion was forbidden, Africans always
respected their enemies' Gods, and because they were at-
tempting to adjust to life here. Jones further observes
that Christianity, through its belief in heaven, took the
slave's mind off the idea of returning to Africa. Also
notes that the emotional emphasis that prevails among Black
churches ie. dancing, is largely a transference from African culture.   (214)

JONES, WILBUR D. "Blyden, Gladstone, and the War." In:
Journal of Negro History, Washington, D.C., January 1964,
pp. 56-61.   (215)

JULY, ROBERT W. "Nineteenth Century Negritude: Edward W.
Blyden." In: Journal of African History, New York, Vol.
5, No. 1, 1964, pp. 73-86.   (216)

_____. The Origins of Modern African Thought. New York,
Praeger, 1967, 512 pp., especially pp. 208-233.   (217)

KEIL, CHARLES. Urban Blues. Chicago, Ill., University of
Chicago Press, 1966, 231 pp. Fine book that focuses pri-
marily on the structure, dynamics, and world of jazz.
Though Keil does not dwell very much on Afro-Americans and

Africa, a number of statements are scattered throughout the
text and the Book is worthwhile for these alone. Some examples: "West African music and European folk music are
enough alike to blend easily into a seemingly infinite array
of hybrids." (p. 30); "in the blending process, the African
rhythmic foundation absorbs and transforms the European
elements." (p. 30); "The great flexibility or bending capa-
city of Afro-American musical forms derives primarily from
a rhythmic superstructure that can incorporate with ease the
most diverse (in this case, European) melodic and harmonic
resources." (218)

KIJEMBE, ADHAMA O. "Swahili and Black Americans." In:
Negro Digest, Chicago, Ill., July 1969, pp. 4-8. Written
by a freelance Afro-American writer who learned Swahili,
this article supports its use among Black Americans, caution-
ing, however, that it will not solve the problems facing
Blacks in this country: "It is no more nor any less than
any other foreign language." (p. 6). In response to various
questions that have been raised about Swahili's suitability
as a language for the Afro-American community, Kijembe says
that though it is not a West African language, it is most
definitely a Black language and that while the slave traders
used Swahili, they also taked in Spanish, German, and other
tongues. Finally, the fact that Swahili was influenced by
Arabic is not so crucial since this is true of other African
languages as well, i.e. Hausa. (219)

KILLENS, JOHN O. "Brotherhood of Blackness." In: Negro
Digest, Chicago, Ill., May 1966, pp. 4-10. (220)

KILSON, MARTIN AND ADELAIDE HILL (eds.). Apropos of Africa:
Afro-American Leaders and the Romance of Africa. New York,
Anchor Books, 1971, 458 pp. Excellent anthology describing
and examining the relationships between Africa and Afro-
Americans throughout their history. Indispensable for understanding the development of interest in Africa. Articles
consist of letters, documents, and general statements by
many authors including Crummell, Garvey, Du Bois, Frazier,
Delaney, and Douglass. Considering that this anthology appeared in 1969 it is somewhat surprising that there is so
little from the writings of the 1960s. Such representation
would have enhanced the collection by showing the continuation and proliferation of such interest in the Black community. (221)

KING, KENNETH J. "Africa and the Southern States of the
U.S.A.: Notes on J.H. Oldham and American Negro Education
for Africans." In: Journal of African History, New York,
Vol. 10, No. 4, 1969, pp. 659-677. Well-done, scholarly,
and fully documented article. Acknowledging that others have
already commented on the possible influence of American Negro
colleges on Pan-Africanism, King asserts that Tuskegee and
Hampton Institutes, with their emphasis on industrial and
trade education, had a profound effect on the direction and

development of missionary and educational work in Africa. Author also discusses the role of the British missionary J.H. Oldham and that of the Phelps-Stokes Fund of New York in exposing many colonial officials and missionaries to the methods of the above-mentioned schools. This, points out King, had the effect of importing to Africa elements of the Washington-Du Bois conflicts and of cutting into Pan-Africanism by encouraging a program of submission to white authority. (222)

_____. "James E.K. Aggrey: Collaborator, Nationalist, Pan-African." In: Canadian Journal of African Studies, Ottawa, Fall 1970, pp. 511-530. (223)

_____. Pan-Africanism and Education: A Study of Race, Philanthropy, and Education in the Southern States of America and East Africa. New York, Oxford University Press, 1971, 296 pp. (224)

KING, MARTIN LUTHER. "Let my People Go." In: Africa Today, Denver, Col., December 1965, pp. 9-11. Published version of Reverend King's address at a South Africa rally on Human Rights Day, December 10, 1965. Calls for an economic boycott by the United States and other world powers on trade with South Africa and argues that it should include Rhodesia and Portugal as well. Says Afro-Americans have a responsibility to help their brothers in Africa and calls on sympathetic whites to join in too. Cites positive influence of independent Black African states in giving Blacks everywhere a sense of pride and dignity. (225)

KING, WOODIE AND EARL ANTHONY (eds.). Black Poets and Prophets. New York, Mentor, 1972, 188 pp. (226)

KINNEY, ESI S. "Africanisms in Music and Dance of the Americas." In: Rhoda L. Goldstein (ed.), Black Life and Culture in the United States. New York, Thomas Y. Crowell, 1971, pp. 49-63. (227)

KIRK-GREENE, A.H.M. "America in the Niger Valley: A Colonization Centenary." In: Phylon, Atlanta, Ga., Fall 1962, pp. 225-239. Account of a colonization effort in an area which is located in present-day Nigeria. Led by Martin R. Delaney, famous Black leader of the 19th Century, the mission failed. According to Kirk-Greene (and other historians) its failure can be attributed to the outbreak of the Civil War around the time of the expedition. (228)

KRYSTALL, ERIC R., NEIL FRIEDMAN, GLENN HOWZE, AND EDGAR G. EPPS. "Attitudes Toward Integration and Black Consciousness: Southern Negro High School Seniors and their Mothers." In: Phylon, Atlanta, Ga., Summer 1970, pp. 104-113. Empirical study of attitudes toward integration and Black awareness in a deep-South city. Based on interviews with 506 respondents (240 mothers and 266 students) in 1967, the study concludes that substantial numbers of Blacks favor both integration and Black consciousness and that the two are not necessarily opposites. Students were more likely to want to visit Africa, more likely to think of themselves as possessing an African heritage, and were more knowledgeable on Africa than their parents, although in general, the level of such knowledge was low when compared to the intensity of feeling about the African continent. Other data showed that African dress or hair style is a poor indicator of the prevalence of integrationist or separatist views. Considering how much has occurred in the Black community since 1967, a replication of this study now might prive very interesting.   (229)

LACY, LESLIE A. The Rise and Fall of a Proper Negro. New York, Macmillan, 1970, 244 pp. Excellent autobiographical account of how an upper-middle-class Afro-American discovered and developed his identity. The first half of Lacy's book deals with his experiences in America, the second with his encounters in Africa, particularly Ghana. Africans are frequently seen by Afro-Americans as having inferiority complexes. They are in turn looked upon by Africans as being arrogant. These and other issues such as the one-party system, cultural differences, and ideological issues are all touched-upon in this fast-moving and highly personal narrative. Interesting reading for high school and college youth alike.   (230)

_____. The Life of W.E.B. Du Bois: Cheer the Lonesome Traveler. New York, Dial, 1970, 183 pp.   (231)

LANDECK, BEATRICE. Echoes of Africa in Folk Songs of the Americas. New York, David McKay, 1961, 184 pp.   (232)

LANGLEY, JABEZ AYODELE. "Marcus Garvey and African Nationalism." In: Race, London, October 1969, pp. 157-172. Interesting article about Garvey's influence on the development of African nationalism, particularly the impact of the Universal Negro Improvement Association on Nigeria and Liberia. Langley argues that Garvey was probably of greater interest to Black nationalist groups than Du Bois despite the latter's extensive activity on behalf of Pan-Africansism.   (233)

LAOSEBIKAN, SUPO. "Social Distance and Pan-Africanism." In: Afro-American Studies, New York, Vol. 3, No. 3, 1972, pp. 223-225. Study based on a sample of 100 Afro-Americans that sought to determine their attitudes toward Africa by using the Social Distance Scale developed by E.S. Bogardus. Major finding was that ethnic preference for Africans was second only to Black Americans (out of thirty ethnic groups). This is in contrast to an earlier study done in 1955 of eighteen ethnic groups in which Africans placed fifth behind French, West Indian, Northern whites in the United States, and Afro-Americans (listed here in order of preference). Laosebikan suggests that change in attitude is due to greater contact between Afro-Americans and Africans and because of a tremendous increase in Black consciousness. Author's conclusions

are hardly surprising though, no doubt, valid. Article, as
a whole, is somewhat superficial, especially in its failure
to analyze the positioning of the other 28 groups who appear
on the scale.   (234)

LARSON, CHARLES R. "African-Afro-American Literary Relations:
Basic Parallels." In: Negro Digest, Chicago, Ill., December
1969, pp. 35-42. Although it does not draw any major conclusions, this is a good article that calls for more study of
a comparative nature, of the literary works produced by
members of these two groups. Larson argues that literature
transcends national boundaries and cites numerous examples
from various writings to show how they affected one another.
Says that South African literature, with its emphasis on
discrimination by writers such as Peter Abrahams and Ezekiel
Mphalele is similar in its themes to Afro-American writings.
                                                                 (235)

LEE, DON L. "African Liberation Day." In: Ebony, Chicago,
Ill., July 1973, pp. 41-46.   (236)

LEGUM, COLIN. Pan-Africanism: A Short Political Guide. New
York, Praeger, (revised ed.), 326 pp. While this book does
not concern itself to any great degree with contemporary
problems of Afro-Americans vis-a-vis Africa, some passages
are well worth quoting. After asking whether color is sufficient to form a bond of kinship, Legum says: "It is necessary
first to disentangle the sense of political solidarity from
that of social solidarity. Black peoples have demonstrated
in a political sense that they feel together and aspire
toward common aims; these do not, however, include the desire
to return to Africa." (p. 111). "The experiences of 'strange-
ness' of being made to 'feel inferior and different' related
by American Negroes living in West Africa, applies equally
to Africans from other parts of the continent living and
teaching in West Africa." (p. 111). Author observes that
Black Americans and South Africans have almost identical
feelings of discomfort and both stem from the same general
fact --- namely that their culture is different from those
around them. One wonders what Legum would have said about
the whole subject in 1972, ten years later.   (237)

LE MELLE, TILDEN J. "Black Americans and Foreign Policy."
In: Africa Today, Denver, Col., October 1971, pp. 18-22.
Advocates use of Black power-politics in order to influence
United States foreign policy towards Africa but does not
discuss how this goal might be achieved. Analogy is made
to Jewish lobbying in this country on behalf of Israel to
underscore the point that whites will never act on their
own to help Africa.   (238)

LESTER, JULIUS. Look Out Whitey! Black Power's Gon Get Your
Mama! New York, Grove Press, 1969, 152 pp.   (239)

LEVINE, LAWRENCE. "Slave Songs and Slave Consciousness: An
Exploration in Neglected Sources." In: T.K. Hareven (ed.),

48

Anonymous Americans: Explorations in Nineteenth Century Social History. Englewood Cliffs, N.J., Prentice-Hall, 1971, pp. 99-126. (240)

LIGHTFOOT, CLAUDE M. *Ghetto Rebellion to Black Liberation.* New York, International Publishers, 1968, pp. 126-138 (198 pp.). Marxist looks at the conditions of Blacks here and in Africa. Points out that Blacks in this country need white allies (along class lines) because they are a minority while Africans do not. (241)

LINCOLN, C. ERIC. "The Race Problem and International Relations." In: George Shepherd (ed.), *Racial Influences on American Foreign Policy.* New York, Basic Books, 1970, pp. 39-59. (242)

LOGAN, RAYFORD W. "The Historical Aspects of Pan-Africanism: A Personal Chronicle." In: *African Forum,* New York, Summer 1965, pp. 90-104. (243)

LOMAX, ALAN. *The Folk Songs of North America in the English Language.* New York, Doubleday, 1960, 623 pp., especially pp. xv-xxx. (244)

_____. The Homogeneity of African --- Afro-American Musical Style." In: Norman E. Whitten and John F. Szwed (eds.), *Afro-American Anthropology: Contemporary Perspectives.* New York, Free Press, 1970, pp. 181-201. Study of the similarities in African and Afro-American music by using cantometrics, a method of rating songs within the context of their actual performance to discover and evaluate their characteristics. Approach differs from earlier efforts in the field which analyzed printed versions of melodies and the poetic content of Black and white spirituals. Many of these studies concluded erroneously, in the author's view, that the Black spirituals were variants of white spirituals. Lomax argues that there are, in any event, a good deal of similarities between the music of the two groups. Good article though quite technical. Not recommended for the beginner. (245)

LONG, RICHARD A. "Toward a Theory of Afro-American Dialects." In: *Papers in Linguistics I.* Atlanta, Ga., Atlanta University Center for African and African-American Studies Center, 1971. (246)

_____. "From Africa to the New World: The Linguistic Continuum." In: W.D. Abilla (ed.), *Source Book in Black Studies.* New York, MSS Information Corporation, 1972, pp. 37-45. Technical article about the linguistic structure of African languages, particularly those spoken in West Africa. Author makes the point that despite the existence of different languages in their respective backgrounds, the slaves were able to communicate through the use of transactional dialects that were actually a form of pidgin. Long suggests that many of the linguistic peculiarities prevailing among Black southerners, such as substituting "d" and "t" for "th" are based on

the phonetics of West African languages. We might add here
that those who would attack this assertion by arguing that
the "th" sound is absent in many languages spoken by immigrants to America ie. French, miss the point --- namely,
that Afro-Americans were living in this country under conditions of prolonged cultural isolation and physical segregation from the dominant society.   (247)

LOVELL, JOHN JR. Black Song: The Forge and the Flame. New
York, Macmillan, 1972, 686 pp.   (248)

LYNCH, HOLLIS R. Edward Wilmot Blyden: Pan-Negro Patriot,
1832-1912. New York, Oxford University Press, 1967. 272 pp.
Primarily a discussion of the man's life. The standard work
in the area. Evaluation of Blyden's views on race and his
long and intense involvement in Liberia is especially interesting for our purposes.   (249)

_____. "Edward Wilmot Blyden: Pioneer West African National-
ist." In: Journal of African History, New York, Vol. 6,
No. 3, pp. 373-388. Discussion of Blyden's colonization
efforts to Liberia and a short overview of this important
figure's life. Lynch argues that the idea of a united Africa actually developed in the 19th, and not the 20th Century.
                                                               (250)

_____. "Pan-Negro Nationalism in the New World Before 1862."
In: August Meier and Elliott Rudwick (eds.), The Making of
Black America: Essays in Negro Life and History. New York,
Atheneum, 1969, pp. 42-65.   (251)

MAGUBANE, BERNARD. The American Negro's Conception of Africa:
A Study in the Ideology of Pride and Prejudice. Los Angeles,
University of California at Los Angeles, 1967, 385 1.   (252)

MAYFIELD, JULIAN. "Uncle Tom Abroad." In: Negro Digest,
Chicago, Ill., June 1963, pp. 37-39.   (253)

MAZRUI, ALI A. "Black Capitalism and Race Relations in East
Africa and the United States." In: Afro-American Studies,
New York, Vol. 1, No. 1, pp. 69-77. Discussion of attempts
to solve racial problems in East Africa and the United States
through the promotion of Black capitalism. Although the article discusses, for the most part, both cases separately,
some similarities are mentioned, i.e. lack of managerial tradition. Comes out in favor of capitalism saying it has a
good chance of helping Blacks attain equality especially
since Blacks "have been promoted from the status of a lower
caste to the status of lower class." (p. 74). Mazrui fails
to deal with possible exploitation of the Black community
by Black capitalists. Rather conservative article.   (254)

_____. "Negritude and Negrology." In: Africa Today, Denver,
Col., June-July 1969, pp. 11-12. Reply to a call by Sterling
Stuckey for comparative studies (see number 342). Cautions

against studying about Africa for the sake of improving Black-white relations in the United States. Viewing it exclusively from a comparative perspective may result in a lack of knowledge about Africa in areas of study indigenous to the African continent i.e. economic institutions, changing cultural norms, and other developments. Africa should be analyzed for its own sake and not to promote better understanding between the races, although it is hoped that this will happen.

(255)

MABATA, J. CONGRESS. "Booker T. Washington and John Tengo Jabavu: A Comparison." In: <u>Afro-American Studies</u>, New York, Vol. 2, No. 3, 1971, pp. 181-186. (256)

MBOYA, TOM. "The American Negro Cannot Look to Africa for an Escape." In: <u>New York Times Magazine</u>, New York, July 13, 1969, p. 30. (257)

McKAY, VERNON. <u>Africa in World Politics</u>. New York, Harper & Row, 468 pp., especially pp. 402-407. (258)

MEIER, AUGUST. <u>Negro Thought in America, 1880-1915: Racial Ideologies in the Age of Booker T. Washington</u>. Ann Arbor, Michigan, University of Michigan Press, 1963, 336 pp., especially pp. 54-69. (259)

_____ AND ELLIOTT RUDWICK. <u>From Plantation to Ghetto</u>. New York, Hill and Wang, rev. ed., 1970, 280 pp., especially pp. 2-4; 17-24. (260)

MEISLER, STANLEY. "New York's African Summer." In: <u>African Report</u>, New York, December 1968, pp. 8-12. Interesting journalistic account of an Urban-League-sponsored trip to Africa. The impact of the experience upon its participants, mostly public school dropouts, is evaluated. Includes selections from poems and essays by the participants. (261)

MERRIAM, ALAN P. "Jazz --- The Word." In: <u>Ethnomusicology</u>, Middletown, Conn., September 1968, pp. 373-396. (262)

METCALFE, RALPH H. JR. "The Western African Roots of Afro-American Music." In: <u>Black Scholar</u>, San Francisco, Calif., June 1970, pp. 16-25. Somewhat sketchy comparison of Western African and Afro-American music. Metcalfe finds at least two major similarities: 1. The social context of these songs, i.e. work songs. 2. Similarities in notes, tones, verse forms, call and response patterns. Article is a review of existing research and presents no new material, relying heavily on quotes from other sources. While Metcalfe begins by attacking the work of white scholars in this area, stating: "no man has the right to interpret another man's past." (p. 16), he weakens his point by quoting from the work of various white scholars such as Melville Herskovits and Jahnheinz Jahn. (263)

MOHAMMED, KIMATHI AND MAINA KINYATTI. "We Want Freedom and
Land." In: Black World, Chicago, Ill., August 1970, p.
21. (264)

MOORE, RICHARD B. "Africa-Conscious Harlem." Freedomways,
New York, Summer 1963, pp. 315-334. Good general discussion
of the historical role played by Africa in the social,
cultural, and political life of Harlem. Talks about the
emphasis of the press on Africa, the role of Marcus Garvey,
the reaction of Harlem to both the Ethiopian and Arab-Israeli
1956 Wars. Also evaluates the stress given Africa by various
members of the Harlem Renaissance such as Claude McKay,
Langston Hughes, Countee Cullen, and others. Good summary
of the different Africa-oriented organizations that have
flourished in Harlem from the 1920s until today's times. (265)

_____. "Du Bois and Pan Africa." In: Freedomways, New
York, Winter 1965, pp. 166-187. Account of Du Bois'
involvement with Africa and his influence on it. Period
covered is from around the turn of the century to shortly
before Du Bois' death. Demonstrates how much Africa was
a part of this great leader's life. Shows how the Pan-
Africanism envisioned by Du Bois was the unity of Black
people throughout the entire world. (266)

MORRIS, MILTON D. "Black Americans and the Foreign Policy
Process." In: Western Political Quarterly, Salt Lake
City, Utah, September 1972, pp. 451-463. Points out various demographic factors and identifies domestic preoccupa-
tion with racism by Black leaders and the masses as being
among the reasons why Blacks have not really been able to
strongly influence American policy towards Africa. Says
that unless Afro-Americans exert political pressure, the
United States will not take great interest in Africa. Links
recent civil rights legislation (since 1965) with the greater
attention toward Africa in the past several years that has
emerged in the Black community. (267)

MORSELL, JOHN A. "The Meaning of Black Nationalism." In:
Crisis, New York, February 1969, pp. 69-74. (268)

MOSES, WILSON. "Marcus Garvey: A Reappraisal." In: Black
Scholar, San Francisco, Calif., November-December 1972,
pp. 38-49. Thought-provoking article that is critical of
Garvey. Moses says that Garvey did not build Black pride
--- he merely capitalized on it. Asserts that the disillusionment with Garvey following his conviction may have been
expanded to a generally negative towards Black nationalism.
Argues that Garvey's middle-class origins and his numerous
contacts with whites shows that he was not "a man of the
people." Moses accuses Garvey of having had an elitist
view of Africa as demonstrated by his lack of interest in
the "uncivilized areas" of Africa except to "redeem them."
Concludes that Malcolm X and W.E.B. Du Bois were far more
important nationalist leaders. (269)

MOSS, JAMES A. "The Civil Rights Movement and American
Foreign Policy." In: George Shepherd (ed.), Racial
Influences on American Foreign Policy. New York, Basic
Books, 1970, pp. 79-99.   (270)

MURAPA, RUKUDZO. "Maroons: Mau Mau Predecessors." In:
Black World, Chicago, Ill., July 1970, pp. 33-38.   (271)

NAGENDA, JOHN. "Pride or Prejudice? Relationships Between
Africans and American Negroes." In: Race, London, Vol. 9,
No. 2, 1967, pp. 157-171.   (272)

NEYLAND, L.W. "Africa: New Frontier for Teaching in Negro
Institutions of Higher Learning." In: Phylon, Atlanta,
Ga., Summer 1961, pp. 167-172. Criticizes lack of programs
in Black universities on Africa and proposes the initiation
of films, courses, counseling on job opportunities in Africa
and the like. Article dated by now but it shows how much
progress has been made since 1961.   (273)

OBATALA, J.K. "Exodus: Black Zionism." In: Liberator,
October 1969, pp. 14-17.   (274)

_____. "Home Away From Home." In: Black World, Chicago,
Ill., May 1970, pp. 32-37.   (275)

_____. "Soul Music in Africa: Has Charlie Got a Brand New
Bag?" In: Black Scholar, San Francisco, Calif., February
1971, pp. 8-12.   (276)

OBICHERE, BONIFACE. "African History and Western Civilization."
In: Armstead L. Robinson, Craig C. Foster, and Donald H.
Ogilvie (eds.), Black Studies in the University. New Haven,
Conn., Yale University Press, 1969, pp. 83-95. While this
article does not deal specifically with attitudes of Afro-
Americans its importance lies in its focus on a basic cause
of some of the negative attitudes towards the African continent that existed in the past among many members of the
Black community. It is an essay largely critical of the
interpretations of African history by many European and
American scholars especially in the context of their discussions of Western civilization. Obichere also criticizes
African scholars for often failing to do research on African
history. Points out that much of the writing on Africa is
characterized by the anonymity of specific tribes, peoples,
and their origins. Instead trade names such as Gold Coast
are used. Concludes by arguing that Africans and Afro-Americans are united by Third World interests.   (277)

OFARI, EARL. "The Emergence of Black National Consciousness
in America." In: Black World, San Francisco, Calif.,
February 1971, pp. 75-86.   (278)

OKOYE, FELIX N. "The Afro-American and Africa." In:
Henry J. Richards (ed.), Topics in Afro-American Studies.

Buffalo, N.Y., Black Academy Press, pp. 37-58.   (279)

_____. The American Image of Africa: Myth and Reality.
Buffalo, N.Y., Black Academy Press, 1971, 157 pp.   (280)

OLIVER, PAUL. Savannah Syncopators: African Retentions in
the Blues. New York, Stein and Day, 1970.   (281)

"Organization of Afro-American Unity: A Statement of Basic
Aims and Objectives." In: John H. Clarke (ed.), Malcolm
X: The Man and His Times. New York, Colliers, 1969, pp.
335-342. This document sets forth the principles and goals
of the Organization of Afro-American Unity founded by Malcolm
X in June 1964. Calling for world-wide unity among those of
African descent, the organization combined demands for commu-
nity control by Blacks with a call for the establishment of
cultural institutions aimed at bringing Afro-Americans and
Africans closer together.   (282)

OTTLEY, HERB. "Nation Time or Integration Time?" In: Black
World, Chicago, Ill., July 1971, p. 41.   (283)

PADEN, JOHN N. AND EDWARD W. SOJA. The African Experience.
Vol. II, Evanston, Ill., Northwestern University Press, 438
pp., especially pp. 363-372.   (284)

"Pan Africanism and Black Nationalism are One." In: Africa
Report, New York, January 1973, pp. 34-35. Interview with
Roy Innis by a Liberian journalist. Innis talks about relations between Afro-Americans and Africans, asserting that
light-skinned Blacks tend to be integrationist/assimilation-
ists (the Black Panthers are included in this group) and
that those with dark skin tend to identify with Africa. It
must be added here that the empirical evidence on this question is contradictory. A study by Friedman, et.al. (Number
394) indicates that people who are very dark or very light-
skinned are more likely to identify with Africa than medium-
complexioned people. On the other hand, Pettigrew reports
on a study (Number 290) in which dark-skinned persons were
at least more knowledgeable about Africa. These two studies
do not, of course constitute sufficient evidence to draw
definite conclusions from and, in any case, there is no
justification for the broad generalizations regarding color
made by Innis.   (285)

PASCHAL, ANDREW G. "The Spirit of W.E.B. Du Bois." Part I.
In: Black Scholar, San Francisco, Calif., October 1970,
pp. 17-28.   (286)

_____. "The Spirit of W.E.B. Du Bois." Part II. In: Black
Scholar, San Francisco, Calif., February 1971, pp. 38-50. (287)

PATTERSON, ORLANDO. "Rethinking Black History." In: Africa
Report, New York, November-December 1972, pp. 29-31. Looks
at the current emphases and perspectives on African history

and deplores the disproportionate emphasis placed on studies of Black people and their contributions to ancient Greece and Rome and North Africa. Also questions the stress placed on East African culture. Patterson argues that Afro-Americans should concentrate their energies more on West Africa, where most Black Americans originated and on "the black experience during slavery." Patterson feels that these areas are far more significant for the Afro-American experience than Swahili or the contributions made by Black people to ancient Greek or Roman civilization. (288)

PEASE, WILLIAM H. AND JANE H. PEASE. "The Negro Convention Movement." In: Nathan I. Huggins, Martin Kilson, and Daniel M. Fox (eds.), Key Issues in the Afro-American Experience. Vol. I, New York, Harcourt, Brace, Jovanovich, 1971, pp. 191-205. (289)

PETTIGREW, THOMAS F. A Profile of the Negro American. New York, Van Nostrand, 1964, 250 pp., especially pp. 10-12. General work dealing with the Black experience. Pettigrew reports on a study which found darker-skinned Blacks better informed on Africa and more favorably disposed toward it. Makes the interesting point that, in addition to enhancing Black pride, the rise of independent African states when compared by Afro-Americans to their own situation, may contribute to feelings of relative deprivation. (290)

PIERSEN, WILLIAM D. "An African Background for American Negro Folktales." In: Journal of American Folklore, Austin, Texas, April-June 1971, pp. 204-214. (291)

POINSETT, ALEX. "Inawapasa Watu Weusi Kusema Kiswahili?" In: Ebony, Chicago, Ill., December 1968, pp. 163-169. Discussion of Swahili, the teaching of it in the United States, and its relevance to the Afro-American experience. According to Ron Karenga it should be taught because it is the one language not associated with a particular tribe. Others say it is the easiest African language to learn, more widely translated, and has many more people qualified to teach it than other African languages. Opponents argue it is an East African tongue and that Afro-Americans come from West Africa in most cases, especially areas where Yoruba and Hausa are spoken. Lyndon Harries, head of the University of Wisconsin's Department of African Languages and Literature doubts that the study of Swahili will change the general image, held by many Blacks of Africa's inferiority. This is, argues Harries, because it is Africa's technology that is deficient, not its languages, of which there are about 800 to choose from. It may be noted with respect to Harries's position that language is a particularly important symbol for a people who are not living in their homeland and who seek concrete ways of identifying with their heritage. (292)

_____. "It's Nation Time." In: Ebony, Chicago, Ill., December 1970, p. 98. (293)

PORTER, CURTISS E. "This Here Child is Naked and Free As a Bird: An Annotated Interview with Barbara Ann Teer." In: Black Lines, Pittsburgh, Pa., Spring 1973, pp. 22-45.   (294)

PORTER, JAMES A. "Contemporary Black American Art." In: Joseph S. Roucek and Thomas Kiernan (eds.), The Negro Impact on Western Civilization. New York, Philosophical Library, 1970, pp. 489-506.   (295)

POWER, JONATHAN. "Carmichael Urges U.S. Blacks to Look to Africa." In: New York Times, New York, February 6, 1971, p. 11. Based on an interview in Guinea. Carmichael asserts that his long range goals are to create an atmosphere that will make Blacks see Africa as their home and that will make Africans welcome Black Americans who wish to return to their ancient land. "Pan Africanism is the highest expression of black power. It means one country, one government, one leader, and one army, and that this government will protect Africans all over the world whenever they face racial discrimination and economic exploitation."   (296)

"The Purpose of Black Power." In: Africa and the World, London, November 1967, pp. 19-21.   (297)

QUARLES, BENJAMIN. The Negro in the American Revolution. Chapel Hill, N.C., University of North Carolina Press, 1961, 231 pp., especially pp. 179-181.   (298)

RAWICK, GEORGE P. The American Slave: A Composite Autobiography. Vol. I: From Sundown to Sunup: The Making of the Black Community. Westport, Conn., Greenwood Publishing Co., 1972, 208 pp. Argues that the slaves combined many African elements of their culture with American ones. According to Rawick, from sunup to sundown the slaves worked for their masters and from sundown to sunup they labored to create the "social living space" necessary for their survival. Relying heavily on the slave narratives, this authoritative and interesting book describes and evaluates the social, cultural, religious, and familial life of the slave's life on the plantation, demonstrating the extensive role played by African culture in his daily life. Author makes excellent use of sources to support his analysis. The remainder of the volumes in this series contain the actual narratives.   (299)

REDDING, SAUNDERS. "Home to Africa." In: American Scholar, Washington, D.C., Spring 1963, pp. 183-191.   (300)

REDKEY, EDWIN S. "Bishop Turner's African Dream." In: Journal of American History, Bloomington, Ind., Vol. 54, No. 2, pp. 271-290.   (301)

_____. Black Exodus: Black Nationalism and Back to Africa Movements 1890-1910. New Haven, Conn., Yale University Press, 1969, 319 pp. Analysis of interest in Africa 1890-1910 and the role of the American Colonization Society in

promoting such interest. Excellent overview of Bishop
Henry Turner and Edward Blyden. (302)

_____. "The Flowering of Black Nationalism: Henry McNeal
Turner and Marcus Garvey." In: Nathan I. Huggins, Martin
Kilson, and Daniel M. Fox (eds.), Key Issues in the Afro-
American Experience. Vol. II, New York, Harcourt, Brace,
Jovanovich, pp. 107-124. (303)

REED, HARRY A. "Slavery in Ashanti and Colonial South Carolina."
In: Black World, Chicago, Ill., February 1971, p. 37. (304)

REID, INEZ SMITH. "Black Power and Uhuru: A Challenge." In:
Pan-African Journal, Nairobi, Winter 1968, pp. 23-27. (305)

_____. Together Black Women. New York, Emerson-Hall, 1972,
383 pp., especially pp. 245-283. Although it is not very
rigorous methodologically, this is one of the few empirical
studies that deal with how Afro-Americans perceive Africa.
More descriptive than analytical, the section on Africa
(part of a larger general examination of the attitudes of
Black women) indicated a general lack of interest in and
knowledge about that continent on the part of many women
questioned. Study contains many useful insights and extensive quotes, taken from in-depth interviews but barely touches
on the question of why Black people in the sample did not relate to Africa. (306)

RICKS, TIMOTHY. "Black Revolution: A Matter of Definition."
In: American Behavioral Scientist, Beverly Hills, Calif.,
March-April 1969, pp. 21-26. Examination of the Black Movement
of the 1960s as a decolonization movement and a comparison of
it with African decolonization. Points out that in Africa
whites invaded and conquered Blacks on their own land while
in the United States whites brought Blacks here against their
will and treated them as a colonized group (enslavement followed by economic, social, and political subjugation). Ricks
asserts that the African revolution is basically one of color
not class. Argues that, as opposed to Africans, American
Blacks are a minority and that they must therefore develop a
strategy which recognizes the difficulty of throwing out the
oppressor as has happened in Africa. This is not to say,
observes Ricks, that the violent tactics employed in Africa
cannot be used in the United States. Rather, they must be
accompanied by an awareness of the risks involved. (307)

ROBERTS, JOHN S. Black Music of Two Worlds. New York, Praeger,
1972, 286 pp. (308)

ROBINSON, RANDALL. "Southern Africa: A Role for Africans in
the United States." In: Black World, Chicago, Ill., July
1971, pp. 34-41. (309)

ROGERS, JOEL A. Africa's Gift to America. New York, Helga
M. Rogers, rev. ed., 1961, 272 pp. (310)

ROSS, RED. "Black Americans and Italo-Ethiopian Relief."
In: Ethiopian Observer, Addis Ababa, Vol. 15, No. 2, 1972,
pp. 122-131.   (311)

ROUCEK, JOSEPH S. "The Black American and the New Viewpoints
in Black American History." In: Joseph S. Roucek and
Thomas Kiernan (eds.), The Negro Impact on Western Civilization, New York, Philosophical Library, 1970, pp. 1-22.   (312)

_____. "The Changing Relationship of the American Negro to
African History and Politics." In: Journal of Human Relations, Wilberforce, Ohio, Vol. 14, No. 1, 1966, pp. 17-27. (313)

ROWE, CYPRIAN L. "Crisis in African Studies: The Birth of
the African Heritage Studies Association." In: Black Academy Review, Fall 1970, pp. 3-10. The African Studies Association is the main organization of scholars (Black and white)
concerned with Africa. In 1969 a dissident group, consisting
almost entirely of Black scholars broke away from the ASA
because of a disagreement over the sharing of power, over how
the ASA was serving the needs of Black scholars and the
community, and the types of emphases placed by the Association
on education about Africa. Article discusses the founding of
the group and summarizes the results of the conference held
in 1970. Its importance lies in the fact that the formation
of this organization is but one example of the development
of Black consciousness vis a vis Africa in recent years.
Twelve years ago such a group might not have been formed. (314)

RUBLOWSKY, JOHN. Black Music in America. New York, Basic
Books, 1971, 150 pp.   (315)

RUSTIN, BAYARD. "How Black Americans See Black Africans ---
and Vice Versa." In: Bayard Rustin, Down the Line, Chicago,
Ill., Quadrangle, 1971, pp. 255-258.   (316)

SALVADOR, G.A. Paul Cuffe, the Black Yankee, 1759-1817. New
Bedford, Mass., Reynolds-De Walt Printing, 1969, 76 pp.   (317)

SCHECHTER, DAN, MICHAEL ANSARA, AND DAVID KOLODNEY. "The CIA
as an Equal Opportunity Employer." In: Ramparts, Berkeley,
Calif., January 1969, pp. 25-33. Among other things, the
authors of this article accuse the American Society of African Culture of having worked with the Central Intelligence
Agency.   (318)

SCHRAG, PETER. "The New Black Myths." In: Harper's, Marion,
Ohio, May 1969, pp. 37-42. Written by a man who perhaps
thinks he will receive credit from others for having "told
it like it is." What his piece amounts to is a condescending
attack on Black identification with Africa that is partoniz-
ing at best. Schrag says that it is ridiculous for Black
people to glorify their African heritage by exaggerations and
adds: "Every black Peace Corps volunteer in Tanzania or
Senegal has discovered that in every respect that matters he

is not an African come home, but an American abroad."
(p. 40). The personal accounts by many Black visitors to
Africa from this country indicate that the author's sweeping
generalization is only true for some, but not all, Blacks.
By labeling this identification part of a Black mythology
Schrag not only shows his ignorance of Africa's history but
also ignores and denigrates its very crucial symbolic value
to Afro-Americans. True, as Schrag says, some Black students
may become bored hearing about Benjamin Banneker and the
"kingdoms of the Nile" (p. 41), but at least they will become aware of their existence.   (319)

SCHULLER, GUNTHER. Early Jazz: Its Roots and Musical Development. New York, Oxford University Press, 1968, 401 pp.,
especially pp. 6-32. Discussion of how the African rhythms
brought over by the slaves developed into early jazz. Reading this book gives one an appreciation of the complexity of
African music. Moreover, it demonstrates how Afro-Americans
simplified their music so as to permit it to blend in with
European influences and styles. Somewhat technical work but
extremely useful in terms of obtaining hard facts about African connections to Afro-American music. One of the most comprehensive and detailed works on the subject.   (320)

SCOTT, BENJAMIN F. "The Technology of Liberation." In: Black
World, Chicago, Ill., July 1972, pp. 29-39.   (321)

SCRUGGS, O.M. We The Children of Africa in This Land: Alexander Crummell. Washington, D.C., Howard University, 1972.(322)

SHALOFF, STANLEY. "William Henry Sheppard: Congo Pioneer."
In: African Forum, New York, Vol. 3, No. 4, 1968, pp. 51-
62.   (323)

SHEPPERSON, GEORGE. "Notes on Negro American Influences on the
Emergence of African Nationalism." In: Journal of African
History, New York, Vol. 1, No. 2, 1960, pp. 299-312. Excel-
lent general history of Black interest in Africa. Interest-
ing section on the triangular exchange of ideas between
Blacks in the United States, the West Indies, and Africa. (324)

_____. "Pan-Africanism, Some Historical Notes." In: Phylon,
Atlanta, Ga., Winter 1962, pp. 346-358.   (325)

_____. "The American Negro and Africa." In: Bulletin of the
British Association for American Studies, London, July 1964,
pp. 52-54.   (326)

_____. "The African Diaspora --- Or the African Abroad."
In: African Forum, New York, Vol. 2, No. 1, 1966, pp. 76-
93.   (327)

SILBERMAN, CHARLES E. Crisis in Black and White. New York,
Random House, 1964, 370 pp., especially pp. 162-188. Much
of this chapter is devoted to a discussion of Africa's past

but some important points are also made concerning the
contemporary scene. Silberman argues that having a past
increases, not only pride, but responsibilities too.
Silberman states that while Africa's past has many positive aspects it possesses some negative ones as well such
as slavery which was merely exploited, and not created,
by white traders. Author takes the position that although
Africa fosters pride and dignity among Afro-Americans it
cannot give them a complete group identity because their
culture is basically an American one. (328)

SINNETTE, CALVIN H. "An American Negro's Reflections on his
Trip to Africa." In: Freedomways, New York, Vol. 2, No.
4, 1962, pp. 487-491. Pediatrician who spent three months
in Ghana and Nigeria urges caution on the part of Afro-
Americans desiring to settle in Africa. Says they must
possess skills useful for developing nations such as busi-
ness and industrial knowhow. Also they should not go there
with the idea of exploiting the economic resources of African lands. Finally, due to the lower standard of living
and the general difficulties in adjusting to a new society,
they must be morally committed to living there. Some ad-
vantages to be gained are pride in one's history and the
opportunity to live in a dynamic and growing society. (329)

_____. "Repatriation --- Dead Issue or Resurrected Alternative?"
In: Freedomways, New York, Vol. 8, No. 1, 1968, pp. 57-63.
Writer suggests repatriation to Africa for those in the Black
community who wish to go. Feels that Black Americans cannot
win a battle in this country as "urban guerillas" because of
their minority position. Nor should they try, says Sinnette,
because it is not their responsibility to reform America.
Sinnette observes that Africa needs people with professional
skills in order to develop. Moreover, the Afro-American
would feel more comfortable in a society where there was no
racial discrimination (This is a simplification that ignores
the existence of other differences, among them tribal origins
and languages). African countries should indicate what skills
they need and recruit people who have them. (330)

SITHOLE, ELKIN T. "Black Folk Music." In: Thomas Kochman
(ed.), Rappin' and Stylin' Out. Urbana, Ill., University of
Illinois Press, 1972, pp. 65-82. (331)

SKINNER, ELLIOTT P. "African, Afro-American, White American:
A Case of Pride and Prejudice." In: Freedomways, New York,
Vol. 5, No. 3, pp. 380-395. Perceptive discussion of some
of the problems involved in how Africans and Afro-Americans
look at each other. While Africans supported the attempts
of Afro-Americans to achieve equal rights, says Skinner,
they may have done so more because fate had determined that
the two groups be judged as part of one larger group, than
out of a feeling that they shared a common bond. Afro-Americans, on the other hand, felt that the existence of independent Black states helped their cause in the United States but

were perhaps also resentful at times about the better treatment often accorded their African brothers who came to this
country. These sorts of conflicts, are, in Skinner's view,
largely due to the role and attitudes of white Americans ---
hence the need to look at all three groups as an interrelated
triad.   (332)

_____. Afro-Americans and Africa: The Continuing Dialectic.
New York, The Trustees of Columbia University, 1973. 37 pp.,
pamphlet. Excellent review of Afro-American-African contacts
and relations from the beginning of the 19th Century to the
present. Talks about Delaney vs. Douglass, Garvey, Du Bois,
and others in terms of their involvement with Africa. The
discussion of the contemporary scene in Africa vis a vis
Afro-Americans is evaluated from the perspective of an insider
who has lived and worked in Africa at the highest level.
Skinner concludes that Afro-Americans today are as involved
as ever with Africa.   (333)

_____. "Policy Toward Africa for the Seventies." Hearings
before the Subcommittee on Foreign Affairs, House of Representatives, Ninety-First Congress, Second Session, March 23,
1970. United States Government Printing Office, Washington,
D.C., 1970.   (334)

SMITH, ED. Where To, Black Man? Chicago, Ill., Quadrangle,
1967, 221 pp. Personal account of a Black American who
worked for the Peace Corps in Ghana. Smith went to Africa
with high hopes but returned disillusioned, concluding that
he felt more at home in the United States. Written in diary
form, the book does a good job of portraying how a sensitive
Black person feels upon making contact with his African
brothers. It also depicts the daily frustrations that built
up day after day. Solid piece of work, whatever ones' position, that has the ring of authenticity to it.   (335)

SMITH, WILLIAM G. Return to Black America. Englewood Cliffs,
N.J., Prentice-Hall, 1970, 167 pp., especially pp. 93-109.
Autobiographical presentation that deals with different aspects of the Black struggle. A novelist and journalist,
Smith writes about Africa, especially Ghana, where he lived
for two years. Emphasized that one of the barriers to the
establishment of rapport between Afro-Americans and Africans
was that Africans saw things (even enemies) in tribal, rather
than racial, terms. Talks about feeling "invisible" and
being a member of the majority. Says that African countries
that were more settled by whites, such as Kenya and Uganda,
have greater empathy for the Black struggle than West African countries who, while they were also controlled by whites,
had fewer whites actually living in them. Despite the fact
that West Africans such as Leopold Senghor stress Negritude,
they are more likely to reflect the viewpoint of the elite
than that of the masses, observes Smith, adding that South
African Blacks are most sympathetic of all to the plight of
Afro-Americans since they are also very much oppressed by

61

whites. According to the author, he was besieged with questions about the Black Movement in the United States by South
African nationalists.

While, as is evident from the above, the pages on Africa
in this account are quite worth while, it is not as comprehensive a work as the one by Lacy (No. 230). In fact, most
of the book deals, not with the African scene, but with the
dilemmas facing Blacks in the United States and in Europe. (336)

SOUTHERLAND, ELLEASE. "17 Days in Nigeria: A Diary." In:
Black World, Chicago, Ill., January 1972, pp. 29-41. (337)

SOUTHERN, EILEEN. The Music of Black Americans: A History.
New York, W.W. Norton, 1971, 552 pp. (338)

STAUDENRAUS, P.J. The African Colonization Movement, 1816-
1865. New York, Columbia University Press, 1961, 323 pp. (339)

STERLING, DOROTHY. The Making of an Afro-American: Martin
Robison Delaney, 1812-1885. New York, Doubleday, 1971,
352 pp. Well-written biography of Delaney. Presents a good
account of his involvement with Africa and his expedition to
the Niger Valley. Highly readable. (340)

STUCKEY, STERLING. "Black Studies and White Myths." In: New
York Times, New York, February 13, 1971, p. 27. Attack on
whites who dominate and control the African Studies Association. Challenges the notion held by some that Black Americans
have played no role in this area by citing the work of Woodson,
Hansberry, and Du Bois. (341)

_____. "The Cultural Philosophy of Paul Robeson." In:
Freedomways, New York, Bol. 11, No. 1, 1971, pp. 78-90.
Excellent article evaluating Robeson's interest in Africa
and showing how he emphasized the importance of knowing
about African culture, dance, language, and African survivals. This greatly expands the general picture of Robeson
the singer and actor, to that of a man greatly concerned
with the Black heritage who was a scholar knowledgeable in
both African culture and history. (342)

_____. "Relationships Between Africans and Afro-Americans."
In: Africa Today, Denver, Col., April-May 1969, pp. 4-9.
Stresses the need for historians and scholars in general
to become more aware of the work done by anthropologists,
folklorists, musicologists, and ethnomusicologists on Africanisms when dealing with the Afro-American experience.
Urges the development of cross-cultural studies of various
aspects of the African and Afro-American experiences. Among
the areas of study suggested by Stuckey are: responses of
Afro-Americans to slavery and Africans to colonialism, the
effect of paternalism on the personality development of
members of both groups, myths, i.e. sexual, developed by
both slavemasters and colonialists, various forms of segregation in the United States and in Africa, demographic studies

of discrimination. In addition, there should be examinations
of the attitudes of lower and middle-class persons on Africa.
(343)

_____. "Slave Resistance as Seen Through Slave Folklore."
In: Inez S. Reid (ed.), Black Prism: Perspectives on the
Black Experience. New York, Faculty Press, 1969, pp. 51-60.
(344)

_____. "Through the Prism of Folklore: The Black Ethos in
Slavery." In: Jules Chametzky and Sidney Kaplan (eds.),
Black and White in American Culture: An Anthology from the
Massachusetts Review. Amherst, Mass., University of Massachusetts Press, 1969, pp. 172-191. Like the work of Rawick
(No. 299) and Blassingame (No. 39), this article looks at
folk songs and tales of the slave demonstrating how they
contained elements of New World and African culture and how
they enabled the slaves to survive. (345)

_____ (ed.). The Ideological Origins of Black Nationalism.
Boston, Mass., Beacon Press, 1972, 265 pp. Important collection of historical documents, including Robert Young's Ethiopian Manifesto which first appeared in 1829 and which urged
Blacks to develop group identity, David Walker's Appeal,
Henry Highland Garnet's Address to the Slaves, Martin R.
Delaney's The Political Destiny of the Colored Race. Also
contains a good introduction by Stuckey to Black nationalist thought in the 19th Century. (346)

SULZBERGER, C.L. "Africa and the American Negro." In: New
York Times, New York, April 18, 1964, p. 28. Argues that
the Civil Rights struggle in the United States is tied in
with the fight for independence and equality in Africa.
Urges Afro-Americans to support African lands by giving of
their knowledge and to work for the prevention of Black
racism in Africa. This last suggestion by Sulzberger is
rather naive for it makes the assumption that Blacks committed to integration will go to Africa as good-will ambas-
sadors for racial tolerance there. Actually, Black Americans
who are least committed to integration would be for more
likely to become involved with Africa. (347)

_____. "An Afro-American Paradox." In: New York Times,
New York, April 14, 1965, p. 40. Again makes the point
that racism everywhere is interrelated. States: "If the
black man in the U.S. does not receive equal rights, the
white man in Africa is doomed to an inferior status on that
emerging continent." Asserts that Afro-Americans should
help Africa financially and should join the Peace Corps.
Claims that these general views were related to him by
Reverend Martin Luther King in a private conversation. (348)

_____. "Memoir d'Outre Tombe." In: New York Times, New
York, April 26, 1968, p. 42. Largely an account of a meeting
between the author and Reverend King in Paris in 1964 after

he had won the Nobel Peace Prize. Discusses King's view
that the racial problems of Africa and the United States
were intertwined and his feeling that Black Americans should
pay greater attention to Africa's needs. Sulzberger argues
that other groups, i.e., Jews, Italians, Irish, etc., also
helped their homelands and that in each instance they did so
before their group had won its struggle here for full equality.
(349)

SUNDIATA, TIKI. "A Portrait of Marcus Garvey." In: Black
Scholar, San Francisco, Calif., September 1970, pp. 7-19. (350)

SZWED, JOHN F. "Discovering Afro-America." In: John F. Szwed
(ed.), Black America, New York, Basic Books, 1970, pp. 286-
296. While being aware of the African heritage is important
for Blacks in this country it has only limited usefulness
in the struggle for equality here, according to Szwed. This
is so for the following reasons: 1. Africa is very complex,
containing within it a multitude of religions, arts, foods,
cultural patterns, and languages that differ greatly from
each other. This can be contrasted with other countries from
which immigrants to America came such as Italy and Ireland.
This makes it difficult for Blacks to develop "a single recog-
nizable package of cultural identity." Writer also says that
Blacks have created a false image of Africa suited to their
needs i.e. Africa was a land of kings, strong armies, and a
single unified culture. 2. The goals and means of developing countries that wish to remove colonizers from their lands
are inappropriate for what is, in Szwed's view, essentially
"a caste exclusion problem." Suggests that Blacks concentrate
instead on fostering close ties with Afro-Americans in the
Caribbean who were also enslaved and brought to the New World
against their will. Szwed points to a history of such
connections as personified by leaders such as McKay, Garvey,
Carmichael, and others.
     The chief merit of this article lies in that it address-
es itself directly to some of the problems faced by Afro-
Americans who seek closer ties with Africa. Yet it can be
criticized on the following grounds: 1. Szwed fails to show
why the existence of many separate culture precludes a positive and heightened sense of identification. Although it
would doubtless be easier to identify with one country, this
does not mean that such a condition is necessary. 2. Identifying with the Caribbean world would essentially leave Black
Americans with the same problems. First, the Caribbean, like
Africa, has a widely differing range of cultures, languages,
religions, etc., although, admittedly, not quite as great.
Second, there are preindustrial and nonindependent lands in
the Caribbean too, thus making their problems as different
from those facing American Blacks as is the case with Africa.
(351)

_____. "Musical Adaptation Among Afro-Americans." In: Journal
of American Folklore, Austin, Texas, Vol. 82, No. 324, 1969,
pp. 112-121.   (352)

THOMPSON, ERA B. "Are Black Americans Welcome in Africa?"
In: Ebony, Chicago, Ill., Vol. 24, No. 3, 1969, pp. 44-
50. Different African leaders are sounded out on their
attitudes toward African immigration by Black Americans
and most are against it. Though the article is probably
dated by now, some of the attitudes expressed by different leaders are revealing. Some examples: Joseph Mobutu
of Congo (Kinshasa): Those "who really want to come to the
Congo to work, are welcome. All need not be talented, but
they must be willing to work - not come to make politics."
Hastings Banda of Malawi: "I don't think they would fit
in; We haven't got a cinema, you know." A positive note
was struck by William Tubman of Liberia: "As long as you
have black skin, you are an African." In Tanzania, where
quite a few Afro-Americans have become citizens, Ebony was
unable to gain access to officials, In Kenya, where a
proposal to give Black Americans and Blacks from the Caribbean automatic citizenship was defeated, a party member
said that part of the problem was the higher income of
Blacks from the United States.   (353)

THOMPSON, ROBERT F. "An Aesthetic of the Cool: West African Dance." In: African Forum, New York, Fall 1966, pp.
85-102.   (354)

_____. "African Influence on the Art of the United States."
In: Armstead L. Robinson, Craig C. Foster, Donald H.
Ogilvie (eds.), Black Studies in the University. New
Haven, Conn., Yale University Press, 1969, pp. 122-170.
Superb piece of work. Presents a great deal of substantive
material that clearly demonstrates the survival of many
specific art forms in the United States. Examples of wood
carvings in Georgia and New York, stoneware from South Carolina, etc., are presented with comments on which parts of
Africa they originated in. Writer's knowledge of his subject is quite apparent in what is possibly the best article
on the topic.   (355)

TOURE, ASKIA M. "Jihad! Toward a Black National Credo."
In: Negro Digest, Chicago, Ill., Vol. 18, No. 9, 1969,
pp. 10-17.   (356)

TURNER, JAMES. "Afro-American Perspectives." John M. Paden
and Edward W. Soja (eds.), The African Experience, Vol. I,
Evanston, Ill., Northwestern University Press, pp. 592-604.(357)

_____. "Black Nationalism: The Inevitable Response." In:
Black World, Chicago, Ill., Vol. 20, No. 3, 1971, pp. 4-13.(358)

TURNER, NAT. "Africans and Afro-Americans and the Word Negro."
In: Negro Digest, Vol. 14, No. 11, 1965, pp. 36-39.   (359)

TYLER, ROBERT. "The Musical Culture of Afro-America." In:
Black Scholar, San Francisco, Calif., Vol. 3, No. 10, 1972,
pp. 22-27. Author is critical of the reduction in "folk

content" of Afro-American music and of the prevailing
commercialism in the world of the Black arts. Says that
spirituals, gospel songs, jazz, etc., are not indigenous
to the African continent but are instead "dialects" of
European music. While there is nothing wrong with that in
Tyler's opinion, he does not feel it should be thought of
as genuine African music. While music in Africa was originally used for different prupuses than is the case today,
its modern forms and uses trace their antecedents to that
tradition.   (360)

"The U.S. Negro in America's African Policy." In: Africa
Confidential, London, June 1962, pp. 5-7.   (361)

ULANSKY, GENE. "Mbari --- the Missing Link." In: Phylon,
Atlanta, Ga., Vol. 26, No. 3, 1965, pp. 247-254. How
Blacks can best identify with Africa is the topic here.
Author rejects emigration as a solution, arguing that the
socialization experience of Afro-Americans is too different
from that of Africans. After noting that Western society
contains within it many features of African art and music,
Ulansky suggests that cultural amalgamation is the answer.
In other words, Blacks will become genuinely Afro-American
by infusing American society with African culture, thereby
making a lasting contribution. In Ulansky's view, Mbari,
the Nigerian-based art club, is seen as a good medium for
exchanges between Afro-Americans and Africans.   (362)

ULLMAN, VICTOR. Martin R. Delaney: The Beginnings of Black
Nationalism. Boston, Mass., Beacon Press, 1971, 534 pp.
This biography is an important source for information about
Delaney. Well written but not as fully documented as
possible.   (363)

UYA, OKON E. (ed.). Black Brotherhood: Afro-Americans and
Africa. Lexington, Mass., D.C. Heath, 1971. One of three
known collections to focus exclusively on the topic (The
others are Davis, No. 97, and Kilson and Hill, No. 221).
Selections are good but dated in some cases and are all
well-known and have been widely published. The focus is
historical with nothing on contemporary politics except
articles by Drake and Essien-Udom, and absolutely nothing
on art, music, linguistics, and social science.   (364)

VANSERTIMA, IVAN. "African Linguistic and Mythological
Structures in the New World." In: Rhoda L. Goldstein (ed.),
Black Life and Culture in the United States. New York,
Thomas Y. Crowell, 1971, pp. 12-35. Discussion of Africanisms that are present in the English spoken by Black
people in the New World. Notes various similarities in
the grammatical structure of African languages and "Black
English", in addition to pointing out the usual words of
African origin. Attacks Crowley's article (No. 91) which
attempts to trace folktales to a single origin and which
concludes that many African tales originated in Europe.

Says that despite similarities in tale-types, they might
have developed out of the human experience independently
of each other and the similarities may therefore be coincidental. Mentions that many Blacks came from the lower
Congo, not West Africa and this may account for the proliferation of East African and Bantu folktales in the United
States. Adds that Anansi and other West African figures
are more common in the Caribbean and that the West African
land of Guinea was a transfer point for peoples from all
over Africa. Vansertima also criticizes other folktale
interpreters and discusses other folktales brought to the
West. Interesting article. (365)

VINCENT, THEODORE G. Black Power and the Garvey Movement.
Berkeley, Calif., 1970, 299 pp. Good biography of Garvey
that contains an especially interesting section on the
Universal Negro Improvement Association's influence on
later nationalism (pp. 217-248). Also discusses how the
Garveyites and leaders of the U.N.I.A. adjusted after the
movement collapsed, what groups they joined, and how effective they were. (366)

WAHLE, KATHERINE O. "Alexander Crummell: Black Evangelist
and Pan-Negro Patriot." In: Phylon, Atlanta, Ga., Vol. 29,
No. 4, 1968, pp. 388-395. Fine, yet brief, article for those
who want a general overview of this missionary who was an
articulate spokesman for Black nationalism. Crummell advocated emigration to Liberia, urged settlers to educate the
tribesmen there, build roads in the hinterland, and help them
economically in other ways. (367)

WAIGUCHU, JULIUS M. "Black Heritage: Of Genetics, Environment,
and Continuity." In: Rhoda L. Goldstein (ed.), Black Life
and Culture in the United States. New York, Thomas Y.
Crowell, 1971, pp. 64-86. Takes the position that both culture and genetics have played a role in the survival of Africanisms. The author states this as a bald assertion, offer-
ing no evidence to back it up other than a few quotes from
Rene Dubos and Siegfried Mandel. The fact that there are
similarities between Afro-Americans and Africans could be due
to culture alone. Would the writer, a Kenyan, exclude light-
skinned Afro-Americans who may be 60-80% "white?" Superficial
piece of work. (368)

WALDEN, DANIEL AND KENNETH WYLIE. "W.E.B. Du Bois: Pan-Africanism's Intellectual Father." In: Journal of Human Relations, Wilberforce, Ohio, Vol. 14, No. 1, 1966, pp. 28-41.
Well-written and concise examination of Du Bois' early involvement in Pan-Africanism, especially the various congresses that were held in those years. (369)

WALKER, SHEILA. "Black English." In: Black World, Chicago,
Ill., Vol. 20, No. 8, 1971, pp. 4-16. (370)

WALTERS, RONALD. "Pan-Africanism: Africa and the Diaspora."
In: Black Lines, Pittsburgh, Pa., Vol. 1, No. 3, 1971.

Call for integrating Afro-Americans into the Pan-African
movement. Acknowledging that there are many differences
between various groups of Blacks throughout the world,
Walters argues that they do have the following in common:
1. Similar understanding of, and experience with, racism.
2. Common racial origins. 3. Differing lifestyles because
of the common need to adapt in order to survive. Points
out that there are large numbers of Africans living in the
United States and that if Black Americans are serious about
developing ties with Africa, they should start by working
and affiliating with them wherever they reside, be it Harlem
or college towns. Black stores should stock African foods,
and Blacks should invite Africans to stay with them. Finally,
Afro-Americans should become more involved with the political
struggles of Africans. (371)

WALTON, ORTIZ. Music: Black, White and Blue. New York,
William Morrow, 1972, 180 pp. (372)

WATERMAN, RICHARD A. "On Flogging a Dead Horse: Lessons
From the Africanisms Controversy." In: Ethnomusicology,
Middletown, Conn., Vol. 7, No. 2, 1963, pp. 83-87. (373)

WEINSTEIN, JAMES. "Black Nationalism: The Early Debate."
In: Studies on the Left, New York, Summer 1964, pp. 50-
58. (374)

WEISBORD, ROBERT G. "Africa, Africans, and the Afro-American:
Images and Identities in Transition." In: Race, London,
Vol. 10, No. 3, 1969, pp. 305-321. Basically a general
introduction to the topic of interest in Africa by Afro-
Americans as manifested in speeches, books, organizational
resolutions. Covers a lot of ground and is best suited for
the reader who has no knowledge of the subject. (375)

_____. "The Back to Africa Idea." In: History Today, London,
Vol. 18, No. 1, 1968, pp. 30-37. (376)

_____. Black America and the Italian-Ethiopian Crisis: An
Episode in Pan-Negroism." In: The Historian, West Melbourne,
Australia, Vol. 34, No. 2, 1972, pp. 230-241. Fascinating
account of the Afro-American community's involvement with
Ethiopia. In addition to discussing the war itself, Weisbord
dwells at length upon the specific interest in Ethiopia prior
to the war, thus demonstrating the historical background to
the support for Ethiopia that emerged full-blown in October
1935. Observes that Ethiopia's special place in the heart
and mind of the Black community was due largely to two factors: 1. Its ancient cultural tradition. 2. Its strong
resistance to European efforts to conquer and colonize it.
Highly readable, informative, and well-documented. (377)

_____. Ebony Kinship: Africa, Africans, and the Afro-American.
Westport, Conn., Greenwood Press, 1973, 256 pp. Excellent
book on the history of African-Afro-American relationships,

primarily in the 20th Century. Contains chapters on Garvey,
Ethiopia, and a particularly intriguing examination of the
many, but little-known, Africanist groups that sprang up in
the years following Garvey's demise i.e. The Negro Nationalist Movement, African Nationalist Pioneer Movement, etc..
Also evaluates current interest in Africa and the attitudes
of Africans toward such interest. Finally, the first chapter
consists of a good summary of the development of interest in
Africa during the 19th Century.   (378)

WEST, RICHARD. Back to Africa: A History of Sierra Leone and
Liberia. London, 1970, 357 pp.   (379)

WILLIAMS, JOHN A. "Open Letter to an African." In: Negro
Digest, Chicago, Ill., Vol. 14, No. 11, 1965, p. 22.   (380)

WILLIAMS, WALTER L. "Black American Attitudes Toward Africa,
1877-1900." In: Pan African Journal, Nairobi, Vol. 4,
No. 2, 1971, pp. 173-194.   (381)

WILSON, ANGENE. "Africa, Past, Present and Future." In:
Negro History Bulletin, Washington, D.C., Vol. 31, No. 6,
1968, pp. 6-12. Review and critique of the shortcomings
present in textbooks dealing with Africa. Cites various
studies indicating the negative stereotypes that high school
students have developed of Africa. Things are improving, says
Wilson in this somewhat, but certainly not completely, dated,
study.   (382)

WILSON, ERNEST J. "Implementing Pan-African Programs --- Now."
In: Black World, Chicago, Ill., Vol. 20, No. 1, 1971, pp. 34-
41.   (383)

WHITTEN, NORMAN E. "Contemporary Patterns of Malign Occult-
ism Among Negroes in North Carolina." In: Journal of
American Folklore, Austin, Texas, Vol. 75, No. 298, 1962,
pp. 311-325.   (384)

WOLKON, GEORGE A. "African Identity of the Negro American
and Achievement." In: Journal of Social Issues, Ann Arbor,
Mich., Vol. 27, No. 4, 1971, pp. 199-211. Social scientists
generally agree that positive identification is beneficial
for members of minority groups. In this study, using a
sample of eighty sutdents, it was found that the grade point
average of those who identified positively with Africa was
lower than those who did not. Author gives several expla-
nations to account for this: 1. Identity with Africa conflicts with the basic middle-class values of this society.
It is essentially a rejection of those values and is therefore a protest identity. 2. The GPA is partly the result of
the teachers' overall judgement of the student, not only his
or her academic performance. 3. Course content is usually
middle-class in nature and is supportive of middle-class
culture and values. Study also found that more males than
females identified with Africa. Finally, the research showed

no difference between different levels of achievement on
aptitude tests or among socioeconomic variables.
       Study has several weaknesses that are probably most
easily attributable to its exploratory nature and the lack
of data on the subject. First, Wolkon does not deal with
why in high school these students did no worse than those
who identified with the United States. Since this contra-
dicts the GPA findings on performance in college, one wonders
why there is no discussion of this. A longitudinal study
would be necessary to obtain the answer to this question.
Also the representativeness of the sample (remedial students
in a junior college) is, as Wolkon admits, highly question-
able. What makes this problematic is that we do not really
know yet with any degree of certainty what sectors of the
Black community identify most with Africa --- educated or
uneducated?, rich or poor?, young or old?, etc.. In general we need more research of this sort.   (385)

WORMLEY, STANTON L. AND LEWIS H. FENDERSON. Many Shades of
Black. New York, William Morrow, 1969, 388 pp.   (386)

WORONOFF, JON. "The New Pan-Africanism." In: Crisis, New
York, Vol. 79, No. 4, 1972, pp. 127-129.   (387)

X, MALCOLM. (with the assistance of Alex Haley). The
Autobiography of Malcolm X. New York, Grove, 1965, 460 pp.,
especially pp. 343-363. One of the most important purposes
ever written on the Black experience in America, this is
the story of the evolution of a revolutionary from convict
to international leader. For our purposes Chapter Eighteen
is most important for it is an account by Malcolm X of his
experiences, reactions, and thoughts while traveling throughout the Middle East and Africa, especially Nigeria and Ghana.
                                                            (388)

_____. "Communication and Reality." In: John H. Clarke (ed.),
Malcolm X: The Man and His Times. New York, Colliers, 1969,
pp. 307-320. Speech given to the Domestic Peace Corps on
December 12, 1964. Argues that the United States become
involved with Africa after the departure of the Europeans
partly out of fear that Afro-Americans would identify too
strongly with Africa and thus become more powerful in their
struggle here in the United States. The major effect of
Africa among members of the Black community has been, Malcolm.
X says, to give them pride in a heritage of which they had
been ashamed in previous times. Accuses the U.S. of distort-
ing the picture to Africans in terms of how Blacks are treated here.   (389)

_____   "Malcolm X on Afro-American History." In: International Socialist Review, New York, Vol. 28, No. 2, 1967,
pp. 1-48.   (390)

_____. "The Second African Summit Conference." In: John
H. Clarke (ed.), Malcolm X: The Man and His Times. New

York, Collers, 1969, pp. 294-301. Most of the article
(based on a press conference given on August 21, 1964)
consists of laudatory remarks about the efforts of African states to unite and move forward. Also praises Africans for warm reception accorded him as an observer at
their conference and for the Africans' sympathetic reactions
tions to the plight of Afro-Americans. (391)

_____. "Some Reflections on Negro History Week." In: John
H. Clarke (ed.), Malcolm X: The Man and His Times. New
York, Colliers, 1969, pp. 321-332. Malcolm X talks about
the important role played by Black people from earliest
times in shaping history and civilization. Says that the
present condition of Black people is due largely to their
ignorance of their glorious past. Accuses whites of deliber-
ately stressing only the accomplishments of Afro-Americans
in the Western Hemishpere so as to be able to take credit
for whatever Blacks have achieved. Exhorts Afro-Americans
to learn more about their African heritage and its ancient
beginnings. (392)

_____. "Speech to African Summit Conference --- Cairo, Egypt."
In: John H. Clarke (ed.), Malcolm X: The Man and His Times.
New York, Colliers, 1969, pp. 288-293. Address given at a
meeting of the Organization of African Unity on July 17,
1964. Saying: "Our problem is your problem.", Malcolm
called on African states to aid Afro-Americans in their
struggle for equality by asking them to recommend a U.N.
investigation of the problem. Warned against Africa being
sucked in by "American dollarism." (393)

ADDENDUM

FRIEDMAN, NEIL, A. WHITE, AND E. EPPS. "Attitudes of Southern
Black College Students Toward Black Consciousness." In:
Afro-American Studies, New York, Vol. 1, No. 1, 1971, pp.
191-202. Interesting article that comes to a number of
conclusions about Black identity: 1. Males show greater
Black consciousness than females. 2. Lower-class students
exhibit greater Black awareness than middle or upper-class
students. 3. Darker and lighter colored people have greater
consciousness than medium colored individuals. Attribute
this to the importance of color in their lives. 4. Length
of attendance at the college (Tuskegee Institute) affected
Black consciousness. Africa was only one of five items
touched on in the Black consciousness scale. The others
were opinions of Stokely Carmichael, being called Black,
wearing an Afro, views on Black power. (394)

FULLER, HOYT W. "A Haircut in Conakry." In: Negro Digest,
Chicago, Ill., January 1963, pp. 74-82. (395)

STUCKEY, STERLING. "Du Bois, Woodson and the Spell of Africa."
In: Negro Digest, Chicago, Ill., February 1967, pp. 20+. (396)

INDEX

Aggrey, James K.   223

African Studies Association   64, 89, 314, 345

Afro-American Press   61, 189

American Society of African Culture   12-16, 58, 64, 97-98, 146, 221, 318

Anthropology   29, 39, 53, 56, 87, 95-96, 150, 178-179, 204, 214, 227, 240, 244-248, 262-263, 281, 291, 299, 308, 315, 320, 331, 338, 341, 351, 354-355, 360, 365, 368, 372-373, 384

Art   55-56, 178, 214, 295, 355

Blyden, Edward Wilmot   35, 177, 187, 215-216, 249-250, 302

Crummell, Alexander   322, 367

Cuffe, Paul   173-174, 221, 317

Dance   29, 39, 53, 150, 178, 204, 214, 227, 299, 354

Delaney, Martin R.   30-31, 221, 228, 340, 363

Douglass, Frederick   30, 221

Du Bois, W.E.B.   19, 38, 54, 65, 82-83, 108, 111-112, 139, 168, 177, 196, 221, 231, 266, 286-287, 369, 395

Education   78-79, 97, 159-160, 181, 222-224, 273, 382, 385, 394

Emigration   30-31, 41, 45-46, 48, 50, 76, 81, 88, 108-110, 112, 114, 135, 137, 145-146, 151-152, 156, 192-193, 199, 201, 230, 253, 274-275, 296, 300, 319, 329-330, 335-336, 353, 362

Ethiopia   84, 88, 105, 311, 377-378

Folklore   90-91, 115, 291, 341, 343

Garvey, Marcus   32, 54, 120-121, 129, 134, 151-156, 175, 177, 221, 233, 269, 303, 350, 366, 378

Harlem   68, 128, 162, 194, 265

History   4, 6, 19, 30-32, 34-36, 38-39, 41, 44, 54, 59, 63-66, 68-70, 73-75, 78, 80-84, 97, 101, 103-104, 106-107, 111, 120-121, 127, 129-130, 132, 134, 138-139, 146, 151-152, 154-157, 165-166, 168, 170-175, 177, 180, 187, 189, 194, 196, 206, 209-210, 212-213, 215-217, 221-224, 228, 231, 233, 243, 249-251, 256, 259-260, 265-266, 269, 271, 277, 284, 286-289, 298-299,

About the Compiler

William B. Helmreich, assistant professor of sociology at the City College of New York, specializes in Afro-American studies. He has published numerous articles as well as *The Black Crusaders: A Case Study of a Black Militant Organization.*